The Enlightenment and Scottish Literature

Volume One

Progress and Poetry

The Enlightenment and Scottish Literature

Volume One

Progress and Poetry

JOHN MACQUEEN

1982

SCOTTISH ACADEMIC PRESS

EDINBURGH

Published by
Scottish Academic Press Ltd
33 Montgomery Street, Edinburgh EH7 5JX

First published 1982
SBN 7073 0290 0

Printed in Great Britain by
Clark Constable Ltd.,
Hopetoun Street, Edinburgh

CONTENTS

PREFACE

This book is the first of two volumes about relationships between Scottish imaginative literature and the Enlightenment. The second, which I hope will follow in the not too distant future, will be called *The Rise of the Historical Novel. Progress and Poetry* has grown from a lecture given to the 1962 Scottish Universities' Summer School, from the 1967 Barclay Acheson Lectures given at Macalester College, St Paul, Minnesota, from a paper given to the 1970 Symposium on the Scottish Enlightenment held in the University of Edinburgh, and another given to the 1979 post-graduate Seminar in Scottish Literature in the Department of English Literature of the same University. I am grateful for comments and suggestions made on these occasions. My gratitude to Dr I. M. Campbell, Mr D. A. MacDonald, Mr H. L. MacQueen, my wife Mrs W. W. MacQueen, Professor R. Schlapp, and to Professor A. J. Steele is even more immediate. The responsibility for errors and misstatements in the text remains, of course, entirely my own.

The late Mrs A. M. Belfour and Mrs Angela West performed wonders in reducing chaotic manuscript chapters to the decent order of typescript. My thanks to them both.

I am also grateful to the Councils of the Scottish Text Society and the Scottish History Society, to the Scottish Gaelic Texts Society, the Association for Scottish Literary Studies, the Delegates of the Clarendon Press, Oxford, and to Penguin Books for permission to use extended quotations from books which they have published. Mr James Thin has kindly allowed me to reuse some of my introductory material for the reprint of the 1805 *Poems of Ossian* published in 1971 by the Mercat Press.

CHAPTER I

PRELUDE TO THE EIGHTEENTH CENTURY

Dr Archibald Pitcairne (1652–1713) is best known today as the author of a Latin verse epitaph on John Graham of Claverhouse, the "bonny Dundee" of Episcopalian, and "bluidy Clavers" of Presbyterian tradition, who died from wounds received during his victory at Killiecrankie in 1689[1]:—

> *Ultime Scotorum, potuit quo sospite solo*
> *Libertas patriae salva fuisse tuae:*
> *Te moriente, novos accepit Scotia cives,*
> *Accepitque novos, te moriente, deos.*
> *Illa tibi superesse negat, tu non potes illi:*
> *Ergo Caledoniae nomen inane vale:*
> *Tuque vale gentis priscae fortissime ductor,*
> *Ultime Scotorum, atque ultime Grame, vale!*

"Last of the Scots, thy life alone could have maintained the freedom of thy native land: with thy death Scotland hath new citizens, and new gods. Freedom proclaims that she cannot survive thee, nor canst thou survive her. Therefore farewell Scotland, now an empty name. And thou, farewell, mightiest leader of an ancient race, last of the Scots, and last of the Grahams, farewell."

For all its brevity, the epitaph is an important document in the cultural history of Scotland. The subject is not so much Claverhouse as the nation itself at a turning point in its history. The Scottish citizenry, under James VII, the last of the ancient royal line to hold power, had been replaced by the followers of the Dutchman, William II (*novos accepit Scotia cives*). The ancient Episcopalian church had been replaced by Calvinism from Geneva (*accepit novos deos* – the *simulata fides, pridemque renata Genevae/Relligio* of Philip's *Grameid* I.146–147[2]). Claverhouse, the last of the Grahams, a race which had produced Montrose and the Graham who was Wallace's companion, had died attempting to repeat the victory of his eponymous ancestor, Grim, the Caledonian who according to John of Fordun and Hector Boece[3] had stormed the Antonine Wall between Forth and Clyde (Grim's or Graham's Dyke), and expelled these earlier foreign invaders, the Romans. As a consequence of 'all these factors, Scottish liberty which had been re-established by Wallace and Bruce, celebrated by Barbour and Blind Hary, had at last been destroyed. Dryden in his well-known paraphrase caught the classical qualities of Pitcairne's elegiacs, but missed some of the overtones, those especially which depend on a knowledge of Scottish history and legend which in all probability he did not possess[4]:—

> Oh Last and Best of Scots! who did'st maintain
> Thy Country's Freedom from a Foreign Reign;
> New People fill the Land, now thou art gone,
> New Gods the Temples, and new Kings the Throne.
> *Scotland* and Thee did each in other live,
> Nor wou'dst thou her, nor cou'd she thee survive.
> Farewel! who living did'st support the State,
> And coud'st not fall but with thy Country's Fate.

Similar epitaphs for Scotland have been composed on many later occasions, the most notable, as well as the briefest, being Lord Seafield's alleged comment[5] that the Union of 1707 was "the end o' an auld sang". In some degree they are a mere convention. From one point of view Pitcairne's verses are only the obverse side of these others with which Dryden at the end of the century concluded his *Secular Masque*[6]:—

> All, all of a piece throughout:
> Thy Chase had a Beast in View;
> Thy Wars brought nothing about;
> Thy Lovers were all untrue.
> 'Tis well an Old Age is out,
> And time to begin a New.

Pitcairne's lament, however, had substantial cause. One need not accept the Whig view of history to see with Macaulay in how many ways the accession of William II of Scotland to the throne of Great Britain changed the intellectual assumptions of the majority, not merely in Scotland and England, but in Europe and beyond. Much earlier, the Reformation had weakened the Judaeo-Christian, Roman and Byzantine basis of the medieval European synthesis; in Scotland, as elsewhere, the monarchy with its embodiment in a single person of the principles of hierarchy and sacred hereditary power had then become the central hope of many who in Alexander Scott's striking phrase[7], wished "to temper time with trew continuance". The violent expulsion of Queen Mary in 1568, and the justification for it which a shocked Europe received from George Buchanan's *De Jure Regni apud Scottos* (1579),[8] Mary's subsequent execution in 1587, and that of Charles I in 1649, had weakened the synthesis still further. Mary however had been succeeded by her son James VI, as eventually – in Scotland immediately – Charles II had succeeded his father. Had any children of Queen Anne survived her death in 1714, developments might, even at so late a date, have been different; as it was, the Hanoverian succession confirmed the Glorious Revolution and effectually destroyed the basis in experience, as Buchanan, Hobbes and Locke had already destroyed the philosophic basis, of the old world-picture. At that time and in that way were planted the seeds of the American, French and Russian revolutions which eventually produced our world of the late twentieth century.

Dr Craig is surely wrong to suggest[9] that the last development of Jacobitism in the seventeenth and eighteenth century, the 'Forty-five, was "more of an out-break or flare-up, which passed off without seriously affecting Scottish society, than something fundamental in his" [i.e. Walter Scott's] "past". In Scotland and England alike, the outward show of an hierarchical and hereditary society continued long after rational or empirical justification had become impossible. Respectable society as a consequence became in some measure pervaded by elements of guilt and hypocrisy, the final unsuccessful challenge to which was also the final attempt of the *ancien régime* to reassert itself, the 'Forty-five. The cruelties which for almost two hundred years accompanied the subsequent "pacification" and exploitation of the Highlands formed one important basis for the industrial and colonial expansion of Britain in the late eighteenth and the nineteenth century. It is easy to rewrite history in terms of might-have-beens, but as Pitcairne half-realized, the economic and political, as well as the literary and cultural history of Scotland and England might have been very different if Claverhouse had survived Killiecrankie. In the early nineteenth century it was as natural for Scott and Galt to turn to this period, as it was for Stendhal, Balzac or Tolstoy to turn to the period of the French Revolution and the Napoleonic Empire. It had formed the civilization they knew, and even now the effects have not totally subsided.

Pitcairne was not the only one to realize that the death of Claverhouse completed a movement in time. James Philip in the *Grameid* quoted above, drew a parallel between the events of 1688–1689 and an earlier point of crisis, the destruction of the Roman republic and establishment of the Empire during the civil war (49–45 B.C.) between Caesar and the adherents of Pompey. His epic is modelled on Lucan's *Pharsalia*, and in effect William II is equated with the tyrannical usurper, Caesar; James VII with Pompey, and Claverhouse with the exemplary Cato Uticensis:—

> *Victrix causa deis placuit, sed victa Catoni*
> (*Pharsalia*, I.128)

Philip's main theme, like Pitcairne's, is the attempted defence of a free and ancient society against destruction at the hands of internal and external enemies[10]:—

> *Et successoris statuit de jure futuri*
> *Artificum foeda illuvies (mirabile dictu)*
> *Judicis et partes Regni de rebus agebat,*
> *Et Regum, invitis naturae legibus ipsis,*
> *Non interruptam seriem bis mille per annos*
> *Innovat, et solo transfert diademata nutu.*
> (I.628–631)

"And this vile gathering of tradesmen (*mirabile dictu!*) fixed the law of succession, and played the part of judge in the affairs of the kingdom. Though the very laws of nature forbade it, the Convention breaks the succession of kings, unbroken for two thousand years, and by its nod alone transfers the Crown."

Philip may have thought otherwise, but when he wrote these lines it had long been clear to many that, for better or worse, the laws of nature had no great effect on hereditary succession to thrones, that their effective power lay elsewhere. In Scotland, as elsewhere, the Enlightenment was already well under way.

ii

Pitcairne, it should be added, was no mere *laudator temporis acti*. He belonged to the defeated Episcopalian party, whose members had for many years adopted, and with the Glorious Revolution did not abandon, an attitude to Presbyterian orthodoxy reminiscent of Voltaire's to Catholicism in eighteenth-century France. Pitcairne became virtually a free-thinker. *The Assembly*[11], an anonymous comedy of which he is probably the author, written during the 1690's although not published until 1722, anticipates Hume and Burns in its satire on the activities of William II's Presbyterian "new men" in Edinburgh. It forms a more sophisticated companion piece to the better-known *The Scotch Presbyterian Eloquence*[12] (1692). His Latinity links Pitcairne on the one hand to such predecessors as Arthur Johnston (1587–1641), George Buchanan (1506–1582), Hector Boece (*c.* 1465–1536), and the writers of *Epistolae Regum Scotorum* (edited and published 1722–1724 by Pitcairne's protegé, Thomas Ruddiman), whose works had created the reputation of Scottish Latinity in the sixteenth and seventeenth centuries. Almost equally it anticipates the recurrent classicism of Scottish literature and architecture during the following century, a classicism which sometimes at least is a scarcely disguised comment on the intellectual *gaucherie* of the dominant Calvinism. In *The Making of Classical Edinburgh* A. J. Youngson remarks[13]: "Europe is full of beautiful cities. Edinburgh is one of the most beautiful of all. It owes its singular character to the late and sudden flowering of Scottish culture, when, as Balfour put it, a country 'which had done nothing up to the eighteenth century, after the eighteenth century began seemed almost to do everything.'" Pitcairne's work shows that Balfour's statement is at best exaggerated, and that the classicism of classical Edinburgh had a quite perceptible prehistory, and in this Pitcairne's work does not stand alone. This chapter will, I hope, demonstrate that the Scottish Enlightenment was the natural, almost the inevitable, outcome of several centuries of Scottish and European intellectual history.

It is typical of the period that Pitcairne was not only, or even primarily, a literary man. He was a physician and anatomist, briefly[14] in 1692 and 1693 Professor of Medicine at Leyden, where one of his pupils was the illustrious Boerhaave (1668–1738). Pitcairne established systematic medical dissection in Edinburgh. He was also a mathematician of some distinction, who contributed to the method of infinite series and attempted, less successfully, to apply mathematics to medicine. (It was probably in this connection that in 1702 he was so delighted to receive the works of Giordano Bruno from Robert Ramsay, "Provost of the old College, St Andrew's"[15].) After his death, his library was purchased by that enlightened monarch, Peter the Great of Russia, and is still to be seen in Peter's city of Leningrad.

From the point of view of the present study, almost the most important feature about Pitcairne is that he was one of many Scottish friends and admirers of Isaac Newton (1642–1727), on whose work so much of the Enlightenment, on the continent as well as in the British Isles, depends. Newton had published his *Philosophiae Naturalis Principia Mathematica* in 1687. Pitcairne regarded Newton's mathematics with something like veneration, but his religious opinions and Old Testament scholarship affected him rather differently. "I have desired Gregorie", he wrote[16] in 1694 about the Savilian professor of astronomy at Oxford, David Gregorie (1661–1708), "to procure me a scheme of Mr Neuton's divine thoughts, (I hope yee'l not laugh) that I may write a demonstration for our religion" (Presbyterianism, that is to say): "but this will be a tale of two drinks". Fifteen years later he wrote[17] on a dispute between Newton's successor in the Lucasian chair of mathematics at Cambridge, the heterodox William Whiston (1667–1752) and the astronomer and mathematician, John Keil (1671–1721): "Mr Whiston wrote on the way of the deluge. It was a paper given him by Mr Neuton. Mr Whiston needlesslie spoke of other things too. Keil fell upon him scurrilouslie i.e. upon Mr Neuton reallie (this lost him the profession at Oxford) and wold needs prove by geometrie that the deluge was a miracle i.e. That the rules of Attraction demonstrate by Sir Isaac are false. but the ill natur'd curr, thinking to please a popish humour that sticks to some protestant divines, did not see That if Mr Whiston's i.e. Neuton thought was wrong, no deluge could have been. Let the bees see to That, boy". The dismissive proverbs with which Pitcairne concludes both accounts belong in spirit more to the late eighteenth century, or even the period of Bradlaugh, than to the times in which he actually wrote.

iii

Practically, intellectually and imaginatively, the Enlightenment and the improvements which formed its material component, represent the central experience, and controlled much of the imaginative writing of educated Scots in the eighteenth and early nineteenth century. The practical side was the most obvious. By 1800 Scottish society was geared to (and profiting by) the world of the Industrial and Agricultural Revolutions in a way which even the most enlightened Scot of the late seventeenth century could not have foreseen, and some aspects of which he might well have deplored. Largely, however, material improvements had resulted from the application to daily life of new ideas, scientifically developed and given literary expression during the seventeenth and early eighteenth centuries, ideas without which no substantial material developments would have been possible. In any consideration of the period, that is to say, the material, the intellectual and the imaginative (Pitcairne as well as James Watt) must be seen as closely related; any study of the one necessarily involves the other two. In the present work, I attempt to show that the creative work of Scottish writers in the eighteenth and early nineteenth centuries was so shaped by the physical and intellectual achievements of the time as to become virtually unintelligible if studied in isolation from them. For most purposes, no absolute distinction is made between literature in Scots, in English, in Latin or in Gaelic, or between literature written by Scots who remained in Scotland, and by those who emigrated to England or elsewhere. Given an experience of Scotland during a writer's formative years, the language which became his medium, or the place of residence afterwards chosen for himself, mattered relatively little.

In general, the Scottish Enlightenment concerned itself not so much with abstract thought, as with the cultivation of an attitude which saw the mind primarily as influencing, and influenced by, the phenomena of the external material world. The scientific study and exploitation of the world for human benefit was a duty as well as a pleasure. The emphasis is derived, at least in part, from the work of the French *philosophes*, which found its most extended expression in the *Encyclopédie* (1750–1765) of Diderot and d'Alembert. The *Encyclopaedia Britannica* (1771) is the smaller-scale Scottish equivalent of the great French enterprise. Both in turn derive substantially from the intellectual achievement of the seventeenth century, in England especially, and in particular from the practical and experimental philosophies of Bacon (1561–1626), Locke (1632–1704) and Newton (1642–1727).

The major debt, it is important to note, was English rather than continental. English and continental thought developed in ways which, as Herschel Baker has shown[18], differed significantly:—

"Broadly speaking, the seminal minds of the seventeenth century evolved two strategies for the pursuit of natural knowledge, the rationalistic and the empirical. The great continental rationalists best represented by Galileo, Descartes, and Spinoza generally conceived of reality in terms of mathematical relationships subsuming the fluctuations and deceptions of sensory appearance – relationships that could, under proper conditions, be intuited directly by the mind of man and then for purposes of description and explanation applied mathematically to the data of sensation. Their methodology, in short, was essentially deductive and essentially Platonic", (and Pythagorean, one should certainly add), "for they hypostatized a fundamentally rational structure in the universe which the human mind, by rigorous and systematic intellection, could isolate and comprehend. On the other hand, such English empiricists as Bacon, Hobbes, and Locke sought not to transcend sense by a process of pure deduction and intuition, but by purifying and correcting the processes of sensation to find in the systematic observation of natural processes ('bodies in motion') the key to the understanding and thus to the control of nature. Their method, then, was essentially inductive."

Newton certainly was a mathematician as well as an Englishman, but, quite properly, he is grouped by Baker with the empiricists[19]:—

"Unlike Galileo or Descartes he made no use of *a priori* ideas, mathematical or other: the most he would say is that a mathematical procedure is useful for certain kinds of investigation, even though we dare not claim for it universal validity in explaining all phenomena. . . . Being an experimental philosopher he rejected hypotheses as inadmissible, like everything not immediately derived from experiment."

Mathematical investigation, nevertheless, rather than the experimental method, was the great discovery of the seventeenth century[20]:—

"In this, as in so many other things, it was Descartes who spoke for his age, even for his posterity. His account of the impact that mathematics had upon his thinking and his imagination is one of the great passages of European philosophy. On that memorable night of November 10th, 1619, when he first fully realized that mathematics was a superb instrument of natural knowledge, his career, and the career of modern thought, gained a new impetus. Mathematical relationships acquired almost the sanctity of Platonic ideas."

During the seventeenth century a number of Scots made important contributions to pure mathematics, but these contributions, it is important to note, almost always had some immediately practical application to physics or astronomy. John Napier of Merchiston (1550–1617), for instance, developed logarithms, which at once became an essential tool of the working scientist. The titles which he gave to the books in which he published his discovery, *Mirifici Logarithmorum Canonis Descriptio* (1614) and the posthumous *Mirifici Logarithmorum Canonis Constructio* (1620), emphasize his sense of the miraculous powers implicit in the tables; powers which were at once realized by the great German astronomer Kepler (1571–1630), who used logarithms in calculating his ephemerides for 1620, and dedicated the work to Napier. Napier was well aware of earlier continental developments in mathematics, as is shown, for example, by the presence in his library[21] of *De Triangulis Omnimodis Libri V* (1533) of Johann Müller or Regiomontanus (1436–1476), the earliest work devoted solely to trigonometry.

James Gregorie (1638–1675) was[22] "probably the most original and versatile mathematician Scotland has produced". He discovered the binomial theorem independently of Newton, the interpolation formula, a wealth of results on expansions in infinite series, in which he made use of what was essentially Taylor's theorem (first specifically formulated by the English mathematician Brook Taylor in 1712 and published three years later, although its full importance remained unrecognized until 1722 when J. L. Lagrange realized its powers and termed it *le principal fondement du calcul différentiel*), and made many contributions to the development of the differential and integral calculus, "to name but a few items". His *Optica Promota* appeared in 1663, and was followed by *Vera Quadratura* (1667), *Exercitationes Geometricae* (1668) and *Geometriae Pars Universalis* (1668). Even from these titles, with the prominence given to optics and geometry, a tendency towards a mathematics which at least *might* be applied is obvious. Gregorie's interests were in fact practical as much as theoretical. He invented the Gregorian reflecting telescope, and as a result of his tenure of the chair of mathematics at St Andrews, a well-equipped astronomical observatory, operational by 1677 but subsequently neglected, was established there. The method which he suggested for deducing the solar parallax from concerted observations of a transit of Venus was finally put into effect at the transits of 1761 and 1769. He engaged successfully in controversy with the Dutch astronomer Christian Huygens (1629–1695), and with George Sinclair (1626–1696), professor first of philosophy, afterwards of mathematics, in the University of Glasgow, author of *Ars Nova et Magna* (1669), *Hydrostaticks* (1672), *The Principles of Astronomy and Navigation* (1688), and a rather different work, *Satan's Invisible World Discovered* (1685).

A certain aptitude in Scots for the empirical, even if misapplied, had already become visible during the sixteenth century. The poet and historian, George Buchanan (1506–1582) wrote a long astronomical poem, *De Sphaera*[23], in which he opposed the Pythagorean theories of Copernicus (1473–1543), published as *De Revolutionibus Orbium Coelestium* (1543), and the more observationally based work of Tycho Brahe (1546–1601). His opposition is mainly the result of a scholar's conservatism posing as common sense; thus, despite Tycho's *De Stella Nova* (1573), a study of the "new" star, the nova, which in 1572 appeared in the constellation Cassiopeia, he rejected the possibility of change in the regions above the moon. *Coelum immune senectae*, "the heavens exempt from old age", is his rather striking phrase in II.18.. It is interesting that he attributes the theory that the earth moves, not to Copernicus, but to Pythagoras of Samos (6th century B.C.), or possibly to Aristarchus of

Samos, the Greek who in the 3rd century B.C. had propounded the hypothesis, reported by Archimedes in *Sand-reckoner* 4–5, that "the fixed stars and the sun remain unmoved, and that the earth revolves about the sun on the circumference of a circle, the sun lying in the middle of the orbit". Buchanan certainly realized the connection between the new ideas and the ancient heresies which he regarded as long since exploded by Aristotle and practical observation:—

> *Terra igitur nec sponte sua secedere mundi*
> *E media regione potest, nec viribus ullis*
> *In latus impelli potis est, tollive, premive:*
> *Cum sit nulla usquam tantae violentia molis*
> *Moliri quae sede sua per vimque movere*
> *Congeriem terrae possit. Nec rursus in orbem*
> *Se rotat, ut veterum falso pars magna sophorum*
> *Crediderat, Samii jurata in verba magistri.*
>
> (I.320–327)

"The earth therefore cannot spontaneously shift from the middle part of the universe, nor is it possible for any strength to push it aside, to raise it, or to lower it, since there is nowhere a force of such magnitude that it can set the mass of earth in motion from its seat and forcibly remove it. Nor does it wheel back on itself in orbit, as the majority of ancient sophists had falsely believed, accepting the hypothesis of the Samian master."

His reasons for rejecting the theory are many. One is simply an appeal to observation and experience: heavenly bodies can be seen to move across the sky:—

> *Octo igitur solos veterum solertia coelos*
> *Noverat: et varii quot erant discrimina motus,*
> *Aethera coelestes totidem divisit in orbes.*
> *Nec tamen (haec ratio quamvis monstrarit aperte)*
> *Cessat adhuc caecis inscitia mersa tenebris*
> *Oblatrare palam, coelum damnare quiete*
> *Ausa, pigram celeri motu convertere terram:*
> *Cum, quibus indulsit sensum natura videndi,*
> *Quotidie cernant noctis cedentibus umbris,*
> *Mane novo Phoebum paulatim emergere ponto,*
> *Aut velut enasci longinquo ex aequore terrae.*
>
> (II.141–151)

"The art of the ancients therefore knew eight heavens only and divided the upper air into as many spheres as there were distinctions of varied movement. However, although Reason has clearly demonstrated these facts, Ignorance, sunk in blind darkness, still has not ceased to carp openly at them, and has dared to condemn the heaven to stillness, and turn the inactive earth to swift motion, although creatures whom nature has favoured with the sense of seeing, as the shades of night are departing, see every morning Phoebus little by little rising anew from the sea, or, as it were, being born from the distant level surface of the earth."

Buchanan gives precedence however to the argument, superficially in complete agreement with common sense, that the swift movement of the earth round the sun, and on its own axis, would necessarily have dreadful consequences for everything on the surface of the planet. (It should be noted that he makes the earth hypothetically rotate from east to west, rather than, as is necessary for the Copernican theory, from west to east.):—

> *Ergo tam celeri tellus si concita motu*
> *Iret in occasum, rursusque rediret in ortum,*
> *Cuncta simul quateret secum, vastoque fragore*
> *Templa, aedes, miserisque etiam cum civibus urbes*
> *Oprimeret subitae strages inopina ruinae.*
>
> (I.357–361)

"Therefore if the earth, impelled by so swift a motion, were to go to the west and return again to the east, it would shatter everything at once together with itself, and the unexpected disaster of a sudden collapse would overwhelm in one great smash temples, shrines, and cities with their wretched inhabitants."

For Buchanan and the majority of his contemporaries the most difficult aspect of the Copernican theory, and the most repugnant to instinct and tradition, was that the fixed solidity of the earth should not only be in motion, but should move in several different ways at once, the most important being the diurnal rotation on its own axis, and the annual orbit round the sun. Buchanan, it is probably true to say, did not fully grasp that two movements were involved; he seems to imagine a Copernican universe in which earth, absurdly, is the only moving body, with everything else – sun, moon, planets and stars – fixed:—

> *Quid Solem loquar aut Lunam? quid caetera coeli*
> *Sidera, quae peragunt non aequo tramite cursum,*
> *Inque chori ludunt speciem et nunc lumine juncto*
> *Mutua conspirant, spatiis nunc dissita longis*

> *Quaeque suum servant diversa lege tenorem?*
> *Haec si perpetua statione immota manerent,*
> *Non procul a fratris radiis ferrugine vultum*
> *Nunc Phoebe indueret, nunc fratrem admota subiret,*
> *Et trepidum subitis tenebris confunderet orbem:*
> *Nec Sol aestiferi modo torrida brachia Cancri*
> *Scanderet, imbriferos modo declinaret ad Austros,*
> *Nunc medio auratas cum limite versat habenas,*
> *A tenebris paribus lucem secerneret horis.*

(I.396–408)

"Why should I mention the Sun or the Moon, or the other planets which complete their course by varying orbits, and take part in what seems a dance, sometimes moving in mutual harmony of conjoined light, sometimes separated by vast intervals, with each following a complex pattern as it maintains its course? If these did not move but remained stationary for ever, Phoebe (the Moon) would not sometimes (i.e. at full moon) clothe her face with red when she had moved far from her brother (the Sun), sometimes (i.e. at an eclipse) creep up close to her brother and amaze the frightened world with sudden darkness. Nor would the Sun sometimes (i.e. at summer solstice) climb the parched claw of the heat-bearing Crab, sometimes (i.e. at the winter solstice) decline to the rainy South, and now (i.e. at the Equinoxes) as he turns his golden reins at the Equator, separate light from darkness in equal hours."

Individual planetary movements are of no great immediate significance in terms of the diurnal rotation of Earth, and it is this fact, perhaps, which gave Buchanan the idea that in the Copernican model of the universe, only Earth moves. Copernicus of course believed that the Earth simply accompanied Mercury, Venus, Mars, Jupiter and Saturn in orbits of different size round the Sun, and that the Moon moved round Earth. Buchanan lacked flexibility to grapple with such a paradoxical complexity of ideas, and as a consequence oversimplified his approach, and caricatured the theory of his opponents. His views follow a general pattern of the time; as Dr Meadows has noted,[24] "Objections to Copernican ideas fell into two categories. The first opposed rotation of the earth about its axis; the second opposed revolution of the earth about the sun. In fact only the latter motion was peculiar to the Copernican hypothesis: a geocentric system might also possess a rotating earth. But contemporary objections to Copernicanism, as also contemporary support, tended to confuse the two issues." Buchanan with his scepticism was in good company; Francis Bacon, for instance, writing many years after Buchanan's death, had a much clearer idea of what Copernicus actually proposed, but his objections have the same apparently empiric basis, and are put forward with as much conviction as were those of Buchanan.[25]

Buchanan, it has long been clear, in this instance at least chose the losing side in the wars of the mind. Yet he chose it on what seemed good grounds to many, and his poem has charm and imagination, as well as a measure of intellectual power. It was probably for these reasons that Tycho, with Copernicus Buchanan's chief target, had his portrait-bust on display in Uraniborg, the island observatory built to his instructions in the Sound between Denmark and Sweden. This was seen by Buchanan's pupil, James VI, when in 1590 he visited Denmark. The King discussed the work of Copernicus with Tycho but, as is evident from one of the poems written to commemorate the visit, it was not so much theory as practice, Tycho's *organa*, the "tools", instruments, used to carry out observations, which impressed him – a truly British attitude[26]:—

> The glorious globe of heavenlie matter made,
> Containing ten celestiall circles faire,
> Where shining starres in glistring graithe arraide
> Most pleasantlie are poudered here and thair,
> Where everie planet hath his owen repaire
> And christall house, a whirling wheill in rounde,
> Whose calme aspects or froward does declaire
> God's minde, to blisse great Kingdomes or confounde—
> Then, if you list to see on earthlie ground
> There ordour, course and influence appeare,
> Looke Tichoe's tooles; there finelie shall be founde
> Each planet dansing in his propre spheare.
> There fires divine into his house remaine,
> Whome summerlie his booke doth here containe.

The "booke" is *De Mundi Aetherii Recentioribus Phaenomenis*, Tycho's study of the comet of 1577, privately printed at Uraniborg by 1588, but not officially published until 1603. During his visit James probably received a presentation copy. Perhaps from deference to 8uchanan's memory, the astronomy of the sonnet with its ten spheres – the *primum mobile*, the crystalline, and the firmament, together with the seven others which house the planets – is diplomatic; it is easily read in Ptolemaic terms, but does not necessarily contradict the ideas of Copernicus who, like Tycho, accepted the existence of the spheres. Tycho, on the other hand, denied the existence of the crystalline, while accepting judicial astrology, which Buchanan denied, and which James seems to take for granted. James did not lose his interest in astronomy when he moved to London in 1603. In 1619 he received the dedication of a work by Tycho's great assistant and successor at the Prague observatory, Johann Kepler (1571–1630), *De Harmonice Mundi*, in which the third law of planetary motion was established. James invited Kepler to visit England, but without success.

Copernicanism, with its emphasis on the central importance of the Sun, appealed particularly to renaissance Platonists and Pythagoreans, a point driven home by Buchanan when he scornfully indicated that such beliefs had as little basis in experience (or perhaps rather in Aristotelian physics) as had those of Copernicus:—

> *Nec levior fuit in positu telluris et undae*
> *Error eorundem, qui moenia celsa Crotonis*
> *Incoluere sophi Lacedaemoniumque Tarentum:*
> *Quippe nihil toto naturae in corpore claudi*
> *Purius aut melius vivaci semine flammae,*
> *Omnibus unde ortus nascentibus, omnibus auctus*
> *Progenitis, vigilisque ciens praecordia motus*
> *Qui meat in lentos discusso frigore nervos,*
> *Insinuansque animam aeternam per membra caduca,*
> *Conciliat fluxis coelestia semina rebus.*
> *Huic igitur multo visa est dignissima sedes*
> *Arcanum penetrale orbis, mediique recessus:*
> *Unde adyto e sacro partes effundere in omnes*
> *Se queat, ut (si fas parvis componere magna)*
> *Quod vegetat pigros cunctis animantibus artus*
> *Sanguinis et vitae fons cor, de pectoris antro*
> *Vitalem spargit per caetera membra calorem.*
> *Proxima post ignem est illis sita terra, nec unam*
> *Hanc statuere tamen: sed et huic Antichthona terram*
> *Adversam aeternos circum ignem volvere gyros.*
>   *Haec procul a vera quantum ratione recedant*
> *Percipe: nam gravibus cum sit vis una movendi,*
> *Sponte sua ut fugiant coeli convexa, fluantque*
> *In medium mundi centrum: ut terra infima sidat*
> *Sponte sua, et media mundi statione necesse est*
> *Aëre libratum vacuo se fingat in orbem*

(I.416–441)

"As grossly eccentric were the theories about positions appropriate to Earth and Water proposed by the sophists who lived within the lofty walls of Croton and Spartan Tarentum. They held that nothing purer or better than the living seed of Fire had been enclosed in the whole body of nature. This was the source of all birth and all growth subsequent to birth, activating a heart of unceasing movement which permeated the sluggish sinews, once Cold had been driven out, and as it insinuated eternal spirit into mortal limbs, domesticated heavenly seeds in the flux of matter. For this element then, much the most appropriate home seemed to be the hidden depths enclosed at the centre of the universe, from which, as from a holy sanctuary, it could pour itself out to reach every part, in the way (if one is permitted to compare great with small) that the heart, the source of blood and life, which throughout the animate creation enlivens limbs otherwise motionless, spreads its life-giving heat from the cave of the breast through the other parts of the body. For those Pythagoreans, Earth was situated next to Fire, and not this Earth only, they postulated, but opposite to it the planet Counter-earth also rolled in everlasting rotation about Fire.

See how far these ideas depart from true reason, for since there is one impelling force for all the elements which possess weight (i.e. in ascending order of density, Fire, Air, Water, Earth), it is necessary for them to retreat spontaneously from the convexities of heaven (i.e. the weightless, quintessential planetary spheres), and flow to the innermost centre of creation, and for Earth spontaneously to settle lowest of all at the midmost point of creation, and to make itself into a globe poised in empty air."

The first three lines refer to the Pythagorean societies which dominated the Greek cities of southern Italy (Magna Graecia) for many years after Pythagoras himself had migrated from Samos to Croton about 530 B.C. The doctrine of the central fire and Counter-earth is generally ascribed not so much to Pythagoras himself as to his disciple Philolaus of Croton or Tarentum, who was born about 470 B.C. Aëtius, for example, in the 2nd century A.D. comments[27]: "Philolaus teaches that there is fire in the middle lying about the centre, and he calls it the hearth of the whole, the home of Zeus, the mother of the gods, the altar and sustainer and measure of nature. Moreover there is another fire surrounding the universe at the uppermost limit. The middle is primary in the order of nature, and around it dance ten divine bodies: the heaven and the planets, after them the sun, under it the moon, under that the earth, and under the earth the counter-earth. After all these comes the fire which occupies the position of the hearth at the centre". Aristotle sourly remarks[28] on Counter-earth and Pythagorean method: "Any agreement that they found between number and harmony on the one hand, and on the other the changes and divisions of the universe and the whole order of nature, these they collected and applied; and if something was missing, they insisted on making their system coherent. For instance, they regarded the decad as something perfect, and as embracing the whole nature of number, whence they assert that the moving heavenly bodies are also ten; and since there are only nine to be seen, they invent the counter-earth as a tenth".

There is something odd here – even including earth, it is difficult to make the apparently moving heavenly bodies total nine rather than eight. Philolaus appears to classify the firmament of stars as in effect a single ninth planet, a view apparently accepted without question by Aristotle. The firmament may have been regarded by Philolaus as a single rotating shell, pierced by apertures, through which the upper fire shone to give the illusion of individual stars. However this may be, the thought-process of the Pythagoreans, as described by Aristotle, is curiously analogous to that of modern sub-atomic particle physicists in elaborating the theory of quarks[29] – completely alien, of course, to the matter-of-fact and somewhat pedantic minds of Aristotle and Buchanan.

Pythagoras and Philolaus are doubly important because they were regarded as agents through whom Egyptian (Hermetic) knowledge had been transmitted to Plato (and so for the most part to later generations), and therefore as themselves possessing a form of that knowledge purer than Plato's own. (The full sequence of *prisci theologi* is Hermes Trismegistus, Orpheus, Aglaophemus, Pythagoras, Philolaus, Plato.) The Pythagoreans are in fact mentioned several times by Plato, and in the *Phaedo* Simmias and Cebes, Socrates' chief interlocutors, are described as pupils of Philolaus. A Peripatetic whose background was Pythagorean, Aristoxenus of Tarentum (born between 375 and 360 B.C.) is one possible source for the story that Plato plagiarized the *Timaeus* from Philolaus.

Solar theology, as expounded by Plato in the *Republic* and echoed by Cicero in *Somnium Scipionis*, the concluding part of his own *Republic*, on which Macrobius wrote a famous neo-Platonic commentary, was thus regarded as a noble but imperfect reflection of a Pythagorean and ultimately Hermetic original, a reflection however which was of the greatest importance to Renaissance cosmologists. Dr Yates notes[30] that Copernicus "introduces his discovery to the reader as a kind of act of contemplation of the world as a revelation of God, or as what many philosophers have called the visible God. It is, in short, in the atmosphere of the religion of the world that the Copernican revolution is introduced. Nor does Copernicus fail to adduce the authority of *prisci theologi* (though he does not actually use this expression), amongst them Pythagoras and Philolaus, to support the hypothesis of earth-movement. And at the crucial moment, just after the diagram showing the new sun-centred system, comes a reference to Hermes Trismegistus on the sun:

In medio vero omnium residet sol. Quis enim in hoc pulcherrimo templo lampadem hanc in alio vel meliori loco poneret, quam unde totum simul possit illuminare? Siquidem non inepte quidam lucernam mundi, alii mentem, alii rectorem vocant. Trimegestus [sic] *visibilem deum*[31].

There are perhaps echoes of Cicero's words for the sun in that famous Dream, on which Macrobius commented, in this passage, but the main echo is surely of the words of Hermes Trismegistus in the Asclepius".

Even if Buchanan had been able to cope with the apparent outrage to common sense inflicted by heliocentricity, the association of Copernicus with neo-Platonists and Pythagoreans, still more with Hermeticists and magicians, was enough to damn his theories in the eyes of a humanist-grammarian.

iv

Traces of the new philosophy are visible in the work of the chief Platonist and Pythagorean among seventeenth century Scottish men of letters, William Drummond of Hawthornden (1585–1649). The second major collection of his poetry, *Flowres of Sion* (1623)[32], represents the final stages of the ascent of the Platonic ladder to the contemplation of the Idea of the Good and the Beautiful, identified with the Christian God. The previous steps had already appeared in *Poems: The First Part* and *The Second Part* (1616), which commemorates his earthly love for Auristella, and the beginning of his eventual transcendence of that love under the spiritual direction which she gives him from beyond the grave. *Flowres of Sion* continues the process in six stages, which begin with the realization, expressed in four sonnets and a madrigal, of the inadequacy of happiness, beauty and power in this lower world of time. Next (Sonnets v–vii) is the realization of the need for eternal intervention to transmute the inadequacies of the temporal world. Sonnets viii–xvi, Madrigal ii, and Hymnes i, ii and iii, give proof of the intervention of eternal happiness, beauty and power by way of the Incarnation, Passion, Death, Resurrection and Ascension of Christ, and by the exemplary figures of John the Baptist, Mary Magdalene and the Prodigal. The fourth rung (Sonnets xvii–xxvi, Madrigals iii–v) establishes the relation of the immediately present temporal situation to eternal happiness, beauty and power. The fifth rung is "An Hymne of True Happinesse" and the sixth, "An Hymne of the Fairest Faire. An Hymne of the Nature, Attributes and Workes of God". The work ends with Hymne vi, "A Prayer for Mankinde".

The stellar and planetary universe plays a part in many poems of the sequence, but from the point of view of the present study, the most important comes in "An Hymne of the Fairest Faire":—

> Low under them, with slow and staggering pace
> Thy hand-Maide Nature thy great Steppes doth trace.
> The Source of second Causes, golden Chaine
> That linkes this Frame, as thou it doth ordaine;
> *Nature* gaz'd on with such a curious Eye
> That Earthlings oft her deem'd a Deitye,
> By *Nature* led those Bodies faire and greate
> Which faint not in their Course, nor change their State,
> Unintermixt, which no disorder prove,
> Though aye and contrarie they always move;
> The Organes of thy Providence divine,
> Bookes ever open, Signes that clearelie shine,
> Times purpled Maskers, then doe them advance,
> As by sweete Musicke in a measur'd Dance.
> Starres, Hoste of heave, yee Firmaments bright Flowrs,
> Cleare Lampes which over-hang this State of ours,
> Yee turne not there to decke the Weeds of Night,
> Nor Pageant-like to please the vulgare Sight,
> Great Causes sure yee must bring great Effectes,
> But who can descant right your grave Aspects?
> Hee onlie who You made deciphere can
> Your Notes, Heavens Eyes, yee blinde the Eyes of Man.
>   Amidst these saphire farre-extending Hights,
> The never-twinkling ever-wandring Lights
> Their fixed Motions keepe; one drye and cold,
> Deep-leaden colour'd, slowlie there is roll'd,
> With Rule and Line for times steppes measur'd even,
> In twice three Lustres hee but turnes his Heaven
> With temperate qualities and Countenance faire,
> Still Mildelie smiling sweetlie debonnaire,
> An other cheares the World, and way doth make
> In twice six Autumnes through the Zodiacke.
> But hote and drye with flaming lockes and Browes
> Enrag'd, this in his red Pavillion glowes:

Together running with like speede if space,
Two equallie in hands atchieve their race;
With blushing Face this oft doth bring the Day,
And usheres oft to statelie Starres the way,
That various in vertue, changing, light,
With his small Flame engemmes the vaile of Night.
Prince of this Court, the Sunne in triumph rides,
With the yeare Snake-like in her selfe that glides;
Times Dispensator, faire life-giving Source,
Through Skies twelve Posts as hee doth runne his course,
Heart of this All, of what is knowne to Sence
The likest to his Makers Excellence:
In whose diurnall motion doth appeare
A Shadow, no, true pourtrait of the yeare.
The Moone moves lowest, silver Sunne of Night,
Dispersing through the World her borrow'd light,
Who in three formes her head abroad doth range,
And onelie constant is in constant Change.

(181–232)

The material universe beyond the terrestrial globe occupies 52 of the 336 lines of the poem; of these 52, the description of the planets occupies 30 lines. Both numbers have a numerological significance: 52 as the number of weeks in a year, indicates that in the descent from God the poet has at last reached the temporal creation, the duration of which will be a Great or Platonic Year. The 30 lines devoted to the planets corresponds to the "twice three Lustres", 30 years, of the revolution of Saturn, the outermost planet, through the Zodiac (or round the Sun); the Saturnian year includes in itself the years of all the interior planets. The entire poem, as I hope to demonstrate elsewhere, has a numerological basis; it is a "world of Concords rais'd unlikelie – sweete" (29), constructed to parallel in miniature the method by which God, the Fairest Faire, "brought this Engine great to light", and by which he "it fram'd in Number, Measure, Weight" (85–86), a method authorized by such biblical texts as *Wisdom of Solomon* 11.21[33], "Thou hast ordered all things by measure and number and weight" and *Isaiah* 40.12, "Who has gauged the waters in the palm of his hand, or with its span set limits to the heavens? Who has held all the soil of earth in a bushel, or weighed the mountains on a balance and the hills on a pair of scales?"

At a first glance, Drummond's cosmology is almost that of the Middle Ages. The earlier Scottish Platonist and poet, Robert Henryson (*c.*

1420–c. 1490) would have had almost no difficulty in comprehending a description in so many ways parallel to his own, as given in *New Orpheus* and, more figuratively, in the *Testament of Cresseid*[34]. Certain emphases however would have puzzled, and might even have distressed him. Where Henryson, for instance, or Chaucer would have placed the *Primum Mobile*, Drummond puts Nature – Natura, Physis, the goddess of change, generation and decay, attributes which traditionally were excluded from the regions above the Moon, but confined to the realm of the four elements, where they gave rise to the science of Physics or Natural Philosophy. We have evidence in an earlier sonnet (*Poems: The First Part*, Sonnet v, "How that vaste Heaven intitled *First* is rold") that Drummond regarded the apparent diurnal motion of the hypothetical First Heaven (not called *Primum Mobile*), as a problem at least open to discussion and potentially capable of solution. Two solutions, he realized, fitted the appearances; one that the First Heaven each day rotated on its own axis, part of which was formed by the North and South terrestrial Poles; the other, that the apparent motion results from the diurnal rotation of Earth. In the first line of the sonnet Drummond's problem is whether or not to accept the second solution, as later it is whether planetary motions result from angelic or material influences ("By Sprights or Bodies, contrare-Wayes in Skie/If they bee turn'd") – in short, whether the science of physics should be extended to the planets. A solution in terms of physics, incidentally, would certainly imply that Earth itself was a planet possessing its own proper motion, and simply by calling attention to the problems, Drummond suggests that for both the second answer is preferable. He was probably influenced by the *Nova Astronomia* (1609), in which Kepler, the greatest Renaissance mathematician-astronomer had developed a much-modified Copernican and Pythagorean position, in terms of which Earth rotated on its own axis and followed a planetary orbit round the Sun, and had also established the first two of his three Laws of Planetary Motion in terms of which the other planets are, like Earth, physical bodies, which move round the Sun in elliptical orbits, during which they sweep out equal areas in equal times. These Laws induced him to give the work the epoch-making sub-title *Physica Coelestis*, "Celestial Physics", which in Aristotelian terms would have seemed self-contradictory[35]. At one stroke Kepler thus abolished the *Primum Mobile*, and extended the realm of Nature beyond the planets to the fixed stars. The paradox shocked the majority of his contemporaries; the Danzig astronomer Crueger, for instance, remarked[36], "In trying to prove the Copernican hypothesis from physical causes, Kepler introduces strange speculations which belong not to the domain of astronomy, but of physics". If one may judge by his poem, Drummond reacted differently; his introduction of Nature in place of the *Primum Mobile* shows no hesitation in accepting the new ideas, perhaps because they confirmed his intuition that the total world revealed to him by the senses was only a shadow of the ideal world of reality. It is perhaps to emphasise the physical nature of the planets that they are deprived of their traditional names and mythological associations.

A Cypresse Grove, first published as *A Midnight's Trance* in 1619, shows that Drummond knew in some detail what the new philosophy proposed; in particular, that the earth moves round the sun (Copernicus, Kepler, Galileo), that the earth has a magnetic field (Gilbert), that the physical universe is infinite, with stars in motion scattered throughout its extent (Digges, Bruno), that comets belong to the solar system rather than Earth's atmosphere (Tycho), that the Moon is inhabited (Kepler) and that the Sun has spots (Fabricius, Harriot, Cysat, Scheiner, Galileo)[37]. His brief reference obviously owes something to Donne's *An Anatomy of the World*[38], but goes well beyond it[39]:—

> "The Element of Fire is quite put out, the Aire is but Water rarified, the Earth is found to move, and is no more the Center of the Universe, is turned into a Magnes; Starres are not fixed, but swimme in the etheriall Spaces, Cometes are mounted above the Planetes; Some affirme there is another World of men and sensitive Creatures, with Cities and Palaces in the Moone; the Sunne is lost, for, it is but a Light made of the conjunction of manie shining Bodies together, a Clift in the lower heavens, through which the Rayes of the highest defuse themselves, is observed to have Spots."

The effect is depressing rather than stimulating: "Thus, Sciences by the diverse Motiones of this Globe of the Braine of Man" (note the Copernican pun) "are become Opiniones, nay, Errores, and leave the Imagination in a thousand Labyrinthes". *A Cypresse Grove*, it should be noted, is a prose elaboration of "Song ii", the concluding dream-vision of *Poems: The Second Part*, in which he is urged by the spirit of Auristella to abandon the quest for happiness in the lower world:—

> Your soules immortall are, then place them hence,
> And doe not drowne them in the Must of Sense.
>
> (235–236),

and from which he awakens to find himself in "the Gold-smiths World againe" (248). Auristella is firm in her dismissal of the beauty, which she does not deny, of the created universe, save in so far as it reflects the transcending beauty of the Creator:—

> This great and burning Glasse that cleares all Eyes,
> And musters with such Glorie in the Skies,
> That silver Starre which with its sober Light,
> Makes Day oft envie the eye-pleasing Night,
> Those golden Letters which so brightly shine
> In Heavens great Volume gorgeously divine,
> The Wonders all in Sea, in Earth, in Aire,
> Bee but darke Pictures of that *Soveraigne Faire*,
> Bee Tongues, which still thus crie into your Eare,
> (Could yee amidst Worlds *Cataracts*[40] them heare)
> From fading things (fond Wights) lift your Desire,
> And in our Beautie, his us made admire.
>
> (219–230)

By the time he put the finishing touches to *Flowres of Sion*, Drummond may actually have come to welcome a system which banished the discontinuity between the apparent permanency of the visible heavens and the very obvious transiencies of Earth.

The *Primum Mobile* was the outermost of the perfect crystal spheres which in Aristotelian and Ptolemaic cosmology enclosed each other and Earth to form the universe. At a minimum eight others were postulated, the sphere of the fixed stars, of Saturn, Jupiter, Mars, Venus, Mercury, Sun and Moon. In "An Hymne of the Fairest Faire" Drummond lists the planets without naming them, but nowhere makes use of the words "sphere" or "circle". He comes closest to hinting at them in his description of Saturn, but even here, I suggest, his language is deliberately ambiguous – it may be read in traditional terms, but equally it need not be. How unusual this is may be indicated by the fact that when James VI wrote the sonnet to Tycho quoted above, he used almost without thinking such phrases as "ten celestiall circles" and "each planet dansing in his propre spheare". Buchanan's poem is called simply *The Sphere (De Sphaera)*. A century earlier, Henryson[41] had used the same terms:—

> The firmament payntit with sternis cleir,
> From eist to west rolland in cirkill round,
> And everilk planet in his proper spheir.
>
> (1657–1659)

Indeed, Drummond himself uses the words in poems where astronomy is merely incidental, and their absence from the passage under discussion, as from the earlier Sonnet v, is therefore the more striking. Once again, the explanation is probably to be provided by Kepler. The heliocentric universe of Copernicus was still built from spheres, circles and epicycles, but it is impossible to reconcile a planetary Earth moving round the Sun in a Keplerian elliptical orbit with a necessarily spherical universe. The point is not necessarily that Drummond was a committed Keplerian; on the contrary, as will be indicated, he was concerned to keep every option open, and the verbal ambiguity of his cosmology is at least as striking as the Keplerian elements. Unmistakeably however his temperament warmed to the *Nova Astronomia* — he at least wished that the new ideas should also be the true ones.

Ultimately, I think, Drummond accepted the new cosmology, but he disguises the fact in such a way that most of his contemporaries might well have missed it. Nevertheless, in addition to those already mentioned, there are several other indications of his preference. The order of the planets, for instance, is not Ptolemaic but "Egyptian"; that is to say, it derives, Drummond probably believed, by way of Plato, Philolaus and Pythagoras from the Egyptian, Hermes Trismegistus[42]. There are two consequences. As Frances Yates has noted[43], "The cult of Hermes Trismegistus — tended to suggest a different position for the sun to that which it held in the Chaldean-Ptolemaic system, universally accepted in the Middle Ages. The Egyptian order of the planets was different from the Chaldean order, for the Egyptians put the sun just above the moon, and below the other five planets, not in the middle of the seven. – – – The sun, of course, is always a religious symbol and has always been so used in Christianity; but in some passages in the Hermetic writings the sun is called the demiurge, the "second god". In the *Asclepius*, Hermes says:

"The sun illuminates the other stars not so much by the power of its light, as by its divinity and holiness, and you should hold him, O Asclepius, to be the second god, governing all things and spreading his light on all the living beings of the world, both those which have a soul and those which have not."

A heliocentric system was thus likely to attract Hermeticists such as Bruno. Equally, any proponent of a heliocentric system was likely to cite Trismegistus. His importance for Copernicus has already[44] been indicated, and Buchanan of course had recognised at least some of those antecedents of the Copernican system. Drummond admired *De Sphaera*,[45] but his reaction was quite different. His description of the Sun contains clear echoes of the tradition within which Copernicus had operated:—

> Times Dispensator, faire life-giving source,
> Through Skies twelve Posts as hee doth runne his course,
> Heart of this All, of what is known to Sence
> The likest to his Makers Excellence.

(223–226)

Elsewhere in *Flowres of Sion* he used the figure of the invisible central fire as an image of God himself:—

> Beneath a sable vaile, and Shadowes deepe,
> Of unaccessible and dimming light,
> In Silence ebane Clouds more blacke than Night,
> The *Worlds great King* his secrets hidde doth keepe:
> Through those Thicke Mistes when any Mortall Wight
> Aspires, with halting pace, and Eyes that weepe,
> To pore, and in his Misteries to creepe,
> With Thunders hee and Lightnings blastes their Sight.
> O Sunne invisible, that dost abide
> Within thy bright abysmes, most faire, most darke,
> Where with thy proper Rayes thou dost thee hide;
> O ever-shining, never full seene marks,
>   To guide me in Lifes Night, thy light mee show,
>   The more I search of thee, The lesse I know.
> (Sonnet xvii, "Mans Knowledge, Ignorance
> in the Misteries of God".)

Drummond hints several times at the inadequacies of the Ptolemaic system. His treatment of Venus and Mercury as inseparable twins closely linked to the Sun is probably an indication that the reader is to regard those two planets at least as revolving round the Sun. At a minimum, that is to say, he adopts the "Egyptian" (Hermetic) system, actually formulated in the 4th century B.C. by Heracleides of Pontus,[46] in terms of which Moon, Sun, Mars, Jupiter and Saturn revolved round Earth, while Venus and Mercury revolved round the Sun. He may also be hinting at Tycho Brake's system,[47] produced in answer to Copernicus, by which not two but five planets revolved round the Sun, which last in turn, with the Moon, revolved round Earth. But Drummond has no unequivocal reference to either non-Ptolemaic, non-heliocentric system, both of which clash with the Keplerian extension of natural law beyond the planets to the fixed stars. Indeed, although this part of the poem is a description of the material universe, Drummond nowhere gives Earth a definite physical position in relation to the rest of creation; he leaves the point, supremely important as it was to the thought of the early seventeenth century, to his readers' imagination and intelligence. His mere failure to call Earth the centre probably indicates heliocentric beliefs.

The numerological structure offers further confirmation. The total number of lines in the poem amounts ("Number, Measure *Weight*", 86) to three hundredweights – 3 × 112, 336. The first hundredweight ends with the First Person of the Trinity, "Midst, end, beginning, where all good doth pause" (112), and the second begins with the Second Person, the Son:—

> Hence of thy Substance, differing in nought
> Thou in Eternitie thy Sonne foorth brought.
> (113–114)

One might expect that the third hundredweight would in some way begin with the Third Person, the Holy Ghost. In fact it is with the Hermetic passage already quoted about the pre-eminent and creative role of the Sun in the lower universe:—

> Heart of this All, of what is knowne to Sence
> The likest to his Makers Excellence.
> (225–226)

Structure, I suggest, here forces the reader to call to mind, first that the lower world is the sphere in which the Holy Ghost is predominantly active, second the sun-like appearance of the Holy Ghost in tongues like flames of fire at the first Pentecost (*Acts* 2.3.), and third to recognise in the phrase "faire life-giving Source" (223) an echo of the phrase from the Nicene Creed, "And I believe in the Holy Ghost, the Lord, the Giver of Life". Spiritually and physically the cosmos of the poem centres on the Sun.

Drummond was directed towards the new astronomy by way of Plato, Pythagoras and Trismegistus, but this influence may have been strengthened by Calvinist and earlier Scotist insistence on the absolute, even arbitrary, power of the divine will. A system which appeared irrational to men was not therefore impossible to God, nor was the necessary in human terms ever more than contingency to God. It is notable that for Drummond the idea of an infinite universe filled by God at once called up the complementary idea that if God withdrew his attention, the universe would at once shrivel to nothing; infinite and zero are equally potential in the divine will:—

> Whole and entire all in thy Selfe thou art,
> All-where diffus'd, yet of this *All* no part,
> For infinite, in making this faire Frame,
> (Great without quantitie) in all thou came,
> And filling all, how can thy State admit,
> Or Place or Substance to be voide of it?
> Were Worlds as many, as the Raies which streame
> From Heavens bright Eyes, or madding Wits do dreame,
> They would not reele in nought, nor wandring stray,
> But draw to Thee, who could their Centers stay;
> Were but one houre this World disjoyn'd from Thee,
> It in one houre to nought reduc'd should bee,
> For it thy shaddow is, and can they last,
> If sever'd from the Substances them cast?

>   (285–298)

The "madding Wits" are perhaps specifically Kepler and Bruno, one a mathematician and natural philosopher, the other a wizard in the full tradition of Trismegistus and the Cabala. Drummond stands separate from either; he was not a wizard, and as a philosopher he was more concerned with the reality of which the physical universe is a shadow, than with detailed observation of relationships with the shadow. The new cosmology however contributed to his intellectual development and found vital, if guarded, expression in his poetry.

Other features of Drummond's work anticipate the Enlightenment even more directly. He was a social and political historian who saw his main work in this field, *The History of Scotland*, as having a relevance to the troubles of his own age, not least because he saw that a division between Church and State was more than possible; it was, or would be, both desirable and essential[48]:—

> "It is a false and erroneous opinione, that a Kingdome can not
> subsiste which tollerateth two Religiones: Diversitie of
> Religion shooteth not up society, nor barreth civill
> conversatione amongst Men. A little time will make persones of
> different Religiones contracte such acquaintance, custome,
> familiaritie together, that they will be intermixted in one
> Cittye, familie, yea mariage bed, State and Religione haveing
> nothing commoan."

In a small way, his sonnet to Sir John Skene[49] anticipates Montesquieu in recognizing the strength-in-weakness of legal codes, the bonds which hold society together. Sir John Skene of Curriehill, Clerk Register (*c.*

1543–1617) was one of the pre-institutional writers on Scots Law who cleared the ground for Stair in the seventeenth, Bankton and Erskine in the eighteenth, and Bell in the nineteenth century. He published *De Verborum Significatione* in 1597, and in 1609 *The Auld Laws and Constitutions of Scotland*, an edition of the probably fourteenth century collection of laws, based largely on Glanvill's *De Legibus* (*c.* 1187) but also containing some Scottish statutes, usually entitled *Regiam Majestatem*:—

> *To the honorable Author, Sir John Skene*
> All lawes but cob-webes are, but none such right
> Had to this title as these lawes of ours,
> Ere that they were from their Cimmerian Bowres
> By thy ingenious labours brought to light.
> Our statutes senslesse statues did remaine,
> Till thou (a new Prometheus) gave them breath,
> Or like ag'd AEsons bodye courb'd to death,
> When thou young bloud infus'd in evrye veine.
> Thrice-happye Ghosts! which after-worlds shall wow,
> That first tam'd barbarisme by your swords,
> Then knew to keepe it fast in net of words,
> Hindring what men not suffer would to doe;
>   To Jove the making of the World is due,
>   But that it turnes not chaos, is to you.

The sonnet begins with cobwebs and works through an ingenious series of images to the maintenance of created order against chaos. Cobwebs are at once the frailest of barriers and the sign of neglect; even the best legal system is weak, and the Scottish one in addition had been long neglected, until Skene/Hercules brought it up from the darkness of the northern underworld. Even then, it was no more than a series of clay figures (statutes-statues) until Skene/Prometheus gave them life, or than Aeson bent with old age until Skene/Medea gave him a transfusion of youthful blood, and so restored his pristine vigour. The ancient law-givers were the dumb ghosts of dead heroes until Skene/Odysseus, by giving them blood, gave them back the power by which they had overthrown barbarism, at first directly by war, but paradoxically chiefly by entrapping it in a net of weak words, the legal codes of the various early monarchs. God made the world, but the laws, though cobwebs, maintain it in existence.

Like Ramsay, Hume and Burns, Drummond was repelled by the irrational sectarian enthusiasm of the Presbyterian left wing, which he satirized in the world-upside-down figure of "A Character of the Anti-Covenanter, or Malignant"[50]:—

> Hee that sayes that night is night,
> That halting folk walk not upright,
> That the owles into the spring
> Doe not nightingalles outsing;
> That the seas we cannot plough,
> Plant strawberryes in the raine-bow,
> That waking men doe not sound sleep,
> That the fox keepes not the sheep;
> That alls not gold doth gold appeare,
> Believe him not although hee sweare.
> To such syrenes stope your eare,
> Their societyes forebeare.
> Tossed you may be like a wave,
> Veritye may you deceave;
> True fools they may make of you;
> Hate them worse than Turke or Jew.
>
> (73–88)

When in 1633 Charles I revisited his native Scotland, Drummond wrote the verses, more eighteenth than seventeenth century in feeling, in which the king was urged to continue material and other improvements and institute new ones[51]:—

> Raise *Pallaces*, and *Temples* vaulted high,
> Rivers ore arch, of hospitality,
> Of Sciences the ruin'd Innes restore,
> With walls and ports incircle *Neptunes* shore,
> To new found worlds thy Fleets make hold their course,
> And find of *Canada* the unknowne Sourse,
> People those Lands which passe Arabian fields
> In fragrant Wood and Muske which *Zephyre* yields.
>
> (*Jove*, 35–42)

His imagination was struck particularly by the establishment of Nova Scotia, the earlier (1629) and less tragic of the two Scottish attempts at overseas settlement during the seventeenth century. (The second was the Darien expedition of 1698–1700). The colony figures more than once in the *Entertainment*, first as a figure accompanying the allegorical Caledonia[52]. "Neere unto her stood a woman with an Olive-coloured maske, long blacke Locks waving over her backe, her attyre was of divers coloured feathers, which shew her to bee an *American*, and to represent new *Scotland*; the Scutcheon in her hand bare the Armes of new *Scotland.*" Caledonia subsequently refers to her in the verses which she addresses to the King:—

> A *Prince*, that though of none he stand in awe,
> Yet first subjects himselfe to his owne law,
> Who joyes in good, and still, as right directs
> His greatness measures by his good effects,
> His Peoples pedestall, who rising high
> To grace this throne makes *Scotlands* name to flie
> On *Halcyons* wings (her glory which restores)
> Beyond the Ocean to *Columbus* shores.
>
> (*Caledonia*, 77–84)

Obviously the glamour of the unknown, the mystery, for instance, of the source of the St Lawrence, had some effect on Drummond, but equally he saw the commercial possibilities of the timber and musk trade which made Nova Scotia so attractive a bait for Drummond's friend and lesser fellow-poet, Sir William Alexander (*c.* 1567–1640). Nor at home did Drummond wish Charles merely to adorn Scotland with palaces and churches; overseas trade and colonization meant that new harbours were required, and the reference to the bridging of rivers shows that he grasped the importance of good inland communications. The ruined Inns of Science are probably the Universities, perhaps also the grammar schools, the restoration of which to their ancient glories was close to Drummond's heart. He himself was an Edinburgh graduate, whose gift of books marked the effective foundation of the University Library. The "ancient Worthies of Scotland" who appear in the pageant – Sedulius Scotus, Duns Scotus, Bishop Elphinstone, Hector Boece, John Major, Gavin Douglas, David Lindsay, and George Buchanan – are all scholars, historians or poets, many with university associations. Drummond's assessment of the Universities in his own time may be judged from his epigram on St Andrews when Parliament met there in 1645[53]:—

> S. Andrew why dost thou give up thy Schooles,
> And Bedleme turne, and parlament house of fooles?

Drummond saw great possibilities and considerable past achievement in Scotland; the possibilities had in some measure been restricted by the departure of James VI for London in 1603 –

> Ah why should *Isis* only see Thee shine?
> Is not thy FORTH, as well as *Isis*, Thine?
> (383–384)

he cried to the King[54] when he returned briefly to Edinburgh in 1617 –
but they were virtually extinguished by the events of the 1630's and
1640's. His death in 1649 is said to have been hastened by grief at the
execution of Charles I. It is likely that he drew some parallel between
himself and the statesman John Maitland, first Earl of Lauderdale, and
grandson of the compiler of the Maitland Folio Manuscript of Scottish
poetry, who died in 1645. Drummond composed his epitaph[55]:—

> Of those rare worthyes which adorn'd our North
> And shined like constellationes, Thou alone
> Remained last (great Maitland) chargd with worth,
> Second on Vertues Theater to none:
> But finding all eccentricke in our Tymes,
> Relligione in supersition turn'd,
> Justice silenc'd, renversed or enurn'd,
> Truth faith and charitie reputed crymes:
> The young Men destinat'd by sword to fall
> And Trophèes of their countryes spoiles to reare,
> Strange lawes the ag'd and prudent to appall,
> And force sad yokes of Tyranie to beare,
> And for nor great nor vertuous Mindes a Roome,
> Disdaining life thou shrunke into thy Tombe.

Drummond's hopes for enlightenment and improvement had been
built on the House of Stewart, whose early monarchs he had chronicled
in the *History of Scotland*, and he had lived to see how from 1638 onwards
his aspirations had come to nothing. Masson is perhaps over-rhetorical in
his picture of the world as it appeared to Drummond in the last year of
his life, but he scarcely exaggerates[56]: "In 1649, the very climax of
disaster and horror seemed to have been reached. The King of Great
Britain, amid the outcries and protests of the mass of his subjects, and
with Europe looking on aghast, brought to a public death; an armed
democracy in possession of England; the very form of rule that one had
always detested and dreaded most, a rule of a few nobles coerced by a
thousand priests, riveted upon Scotland! It was as if one had lived all this
while only to see the elements confounded, the Earth's basis loosened,
the Heavens hung with black".

Drummond could not have foreseen that eventually the new philosophy, which had excited and depressed him, and the very disasters which had afflicted him, would help to produce some of the changes he had advocated. Even if he had, he might have thought the cost too high.

v

The intellectual achievement of seventeenth century Scotland is more extensive than is generally realized, and here only a few brief indications will be attempted. The historians are reserved for later mention.

James Gregorie was succeeded in the Edinburgh chair by his nephew David Gregorie (1661–1708), a friend and protégé of Newton, who introduced Newtonianism at Edinburgh long before it was taught in England. Eventually he moved south to become Savilian professor of astronomy at Oxford and, no doubt, to bring work at his new university up to Edinburgh standards. His main works were *Catoptricae et Dioptricae Sphericae Elementa* (1695) and *Astronomiae Physicae et Geometricae Elementa* (1702). (The Gregorie or Gregory family came to form a kind of dominating academic and medical dynasty in eighteenth century Scotland. One or two later members are mentioned below.[57])

An earlier physician and Episcopalian, the best of whose Latin poetry outdoes even that of Pitcairne, is Arthur Johnston (1587–1641), M.D. of Padua, who had studied and taught at Heidelberg, and who for nearly twenty years was a professor at Sedan. On his return to Aberdeen in 1622, he became titular Royal Physician, and in 1637 Rector of King's College, one of the two Aberdeen universities. His continental experiences do not seem to have entailed any distancing from his native country; his poetry[58] is primarily Scottish, and indeed primarily North-Eastern:—

> *Haec mihi terra parens: gens has Ionstonia lymphas*
> *Arvaque per centum missa tuetur avos.*
> *Clara Maroneis evasit Mantua cunis,*
> *Me mea natalis nobilitabit humus.*
> (*De Loco Suo Natali* 19–22)

"This is my native land: the Johnstons have held sway over these waters and fields for a hundred generations. Mantua became famous by being the birthplace of Virgil, but to me my native soil will bring renown."

Save for his friend Drummond, Johnston is the most accomplished poet of lowland Scotland in the seventeenth century.

John Arbuthnot, the friend of Pope and Swift, author both of an *Essay on the Usefulness of Mathematical Learning* (1701) and the satirical *History of John Bull* (1727), was the son of an Episcopalian priest in the Mearns, graduated M.D. from St Andrews in 1696, and soon became a fashionable London physician, author and wit.

After the mathematicians, the botanists[59] were the chief Scottish contributors to the advancement of natural knowledge in the seventeenth century. As the titles of their principal works indicate, their aim was Baconian, to "prepare a Natural and Experimental History, sufficient and good". Robert Morison (1620–1683) was a graduate in medicine of Aberdeen and Angers. Between 1650 and 1660 he was one of the three Keepers of the botanic garden of the Duke of Orleans at Blois. At the Restoration in 1660, Charles II made him his senior physician, King's Botanist and Superintendent of Royal Gardens. In 1669 he became the first professor of botany at Oxford. His most important works are *Praeludia Botanica* (1669), *Plantarum Umbelliferarum Distributio Nova* (1672) and *Plantarum Historia Universalis Oxoniensis* (1680).

Morison's work influenced Sir Robert Sibbald (1641–1722), a graduate of Edinburgh and Angers, who with Andrew Balfour (1630–1694) was responsible for the foundation in 1670 of the Edinburgh Royal Botanic Garden, originally called the Physic Garden. In 1681 the Royal College of Physicians was founded in Edinburgh (the Royal College of Surgeons had been founded by James IV in 1506), and in 1685 Sibbald became the first professor of medicine in the university of Edinburgh. In 1684 he published the best-known of his voluminous writings, *Scotia Illustrata: sive Prodromus Historiae Naturalis*. Like Balfour, he left his natural history collection to the university.

In the sphere of legal studies, James Dalrymple, 1st Viscount Stair (1619–1695) produced in 1681 the epoch-making *Institutions of the Law of Scotland*. Sir George Mackenzie of Rosehaugh (1636–1691) founded in 1684 the Advocates' Library, now the National Library of Scotland, of which David Hume was Keeper from 1752 to 1757, and which, with the university libraries, provided the material on which much of the literary and philosophic work of the Scottish Enlightenment was to be based. Mackenzie, it should be noted, had some gifts for imaginative literature; he was the author of a prose romance, *Aretina* (1660) as well as the more philosophic *Religio Stoici* (1663)[60].

Finally, some mention must be made of an aberrant aspect of the movement – the attempted scientific study of the supernatural. This was frequently, but not invariably, bound up with an interest in the notorious witch trials of the sixteenth and seventeenth centuries. The subject was well-established. James VI published his *Daemonologia* in 1597. As late as 1685, George Sinclair, the opponent of James Gregorie, published *Satan's Invisible World Discovered*, a work which remained in popular demand for the next thirty years. More important in human and scholarly terms is *The Secret Commonwealth of Elves, Fauns and Fairies* (1691), written in English by the Gaelic-speaking scholar, Robert Kirk[61]. He was born somewhere about 1640, and died ("if he did die, which is disputed", wrote Andrew Lang[62]) in 1692. He was an Edinburgh graduate, and served as minister, first of Balquhidder and afterwards of Aberfoyle. He was employed on the Gaelic translation of the Bible, and he published a Psalter in Gaelic (1684). The book by which he is remembered is of a very different kind, yet in a real enough sense its proper place is among the books already mentioned in this chapter. For any Gaelic-speaker, the Other-world, and in particular the *daoine sìth* or fairies and the second sight, were at least potentially as much the subject of scientific investigation as any of those proposed in England by the recently founded Royal Society[63]. Indeed, the closest parallel to Kirk's brief work is provided by that of a notable early member of the Royal Society, Joseph Glanvill[64] (1636–1680), especially in *A Philosophical Endeavour towards the Defense of the Being of Witches and Apparitions* (1666), which was expanded to appear posthumously, under the editorship of the Cambridge Platonist, Henry More (1614–1687), as *Saducismus Triumphatus* (1681). Glanvill however, like James VI and Sinclair, was concerned primarily with evil spirits; Kirk with the nature of a particular kind of spirit whose moral status scarcely differed at all from the human[65]:—

> "As to Vice and Sin, whatever their own Laws be, sure, according to ours, and Equity, natural, civil, and reveal'd, they transgress and commit Acts of Injustice, and Sin, by what is above said as to their stealing of Nurses to their Children, and that other sort of Plaginism in catching our Children away, (may seem to heir some Estate in those invisible Dominions,) which never returne. For the Inconvenience of their Succubi, who tryst with Men, it is abominable; but for Swearing and Intemperance, they are not observed so subject to those Irregularities, as to Envy, Spite, Hypocracie, Lieing and Dissimulation."

Fairies have a precise place in Kirk's order of creation; in accordance with the principle of plenitude, they[66]

> "are said to be of a middle Nature betwixt Man and Angel, as were Daemons thought to be of old; of intelligent studious

Spirits, and light changable Bodies (lyke those called Astral),
somewhat of the nature of a condensed Cloud, and best seen in
Twilight – – – There Bodies of congealled Air are some tymes
caried aloft, other whiles grovel in different Schapes, and enter
into any Cranie or Clift of the Earth where Air enters, to their
ordinary Dwellings; the Earth being full of Cavities and Cells,
and there being no Place nor Creature but is supposed to have
other Animals (greater or lesser) living in or upon it as
Inhabitants; and no such thing as a pure Wilderness in the
whole Universe.

We then (the more terrestriall kind have now so numerously
planted all Countreys,) do labour for that abstruse People, as
weill as for ourselves. Allbeit, when severall Countreys were
unhabited by us, these had their easy Tillage above ground, as
we now. The print of those Furrous do yet remaine to be seen
on the Shoulders of very high Hills, which was done when the
champayn Ground was Wood and Forrest."

vi

The emphasis placed by the Enlightenment on the material world
fitted rather easily into the overall tradition of Scottish imaginative
literature. Peace, prosperity and order had always been the objectives of
Scottish policy, but the smallness of Scotland, the existence of two
languages and cultures within the kingdom, and the vicinity of an
aggressive England, had preserved Scots from any delusion that social
stability and material progress formed part of the inevitable order of
things. The Boethian contrast of an orderly material universe with a
disordered mankind had always a particular poignancy in Scotland,
accompanying and arousing the passionate desire for a more common-
sense, a more obviously comfortable and natural, disposition of things
under the moon. In the fourteenth century it was the contrast between
natural freedom and the "thirlage" in which the Scots found themselves
which, according to Barbour, roused Bruce to take up the struggle
against the English king, Edward. Bruce's successes resulted from the
careful and intelligent use of limited material resources towards a well-
defined purpose. The parallel between the success of Bruce as king and
administrator and that of the improving landlords of the eighteenth
century is more than accidental. So too is the parallel between much
Scottish poetry and prose of the eighteenth century and the Manual of
Kingship, cast in romance form which Barbour produced for late fourteenth century Scotland.

Again, in the fifteenth century Robert Henryson possesses a vision, almost Newtonian because Platonic and Pythagorean, of an orderly and comprehensible universe[67]:—

> Yit nevertheles we may haif knawledgeing
> Off God almychtie, be his Creatouris,
> That he is gude, ffair, wyis and bening;
> Exempill tak be thir Jolie flouris,
> Rycht sweit off smell, and plesant off colouris,
> Sum grene, sum blew, sum purpour, quhyte, and reid,
> Thus distribute be gift off his Godheid.
>
> The firmament payntit with sternis cleir,
> From eist to west rolland in cirkill round,
> And everilk Planet in his proper Spheir,
> In moving makand Harmonie and sound;
> The fyre, the Air, the watter, and the ground –
> Till understand it is aneuch, I wis,
> That God in all his werkis wittie is.
>
> (1650–1663)

This image of a "witty" God in his creation he counterpoints with a fable, "The Preaching of the Swallow", about the complacency and frailty of the people who inhabit the orderly universe and follows it by another "The Lion and the Mouse", in which he restates the morality in terms specifically of Scotland. Implicit throughout is the aspiration, also characteristic of the Enlightenment, that Scotland might become a worthy part of the glorious creation.

David Lindsay (1486–1555), in his usual way, is more specific and more limited, and with the popularity he retained until the end of the eighteenth century, it is possible, even likely, that he influenced Allan Ramsay, James Thomson and other later poets. Thomson, for instance, constructed his not very successful *Liberty* (1735–1736) on the plan of a survey of universal history, with the emergence of a united Britain after 1707 as the climax of the entire process. The structure is very much like that of Lindsay's *Monarche*, where the parallel climax is the Protestant Reformation in Scotland – something which was not yet fully under way when Lindsay wrote.

The kinship between Lindsay and the Scots of the Enlightenment is frequently missed because Lindsay laid his emphasis so much on the Protestant reformation as the cure for the ills of Scotland, that he tends to be grouped more with the Auld Lichts and the Cameronians, than with the moderates and seculars. Scottish Protestantism however, underwent many changes and modifications between Lindsay's death and the Glorious Revolution. (Even so, it must be noted, the most extreme Cameronians held firmly to the idea that Scotland must be a model for the entire sinful world – a Calvinistic anticipation of the Heavenly City of the Eighteenth Century Philosophers[68]. The relationship between the Scots *literati* and the Covenanters is closer than one might immediately suspect). Elsewhere I have emphasized[69] the extent to which the entire early Reformation was a movement towards an apparent rationality, and have quoted Lindsay and Alexander Scott in support of the view. In the context of eighteenth century developments, the extent to which both were concerned with material prosperity and development is most striking. For Lindsay, in the *Dreme*[70] the combination in Scotland of potential abundance and actual poverty is inexplicable:—

> Quhen that I had oversene this Regioun,
> The quhilk, of nature, is boith gude and fair,
> I did propone ane lytill questioun,
> Beseikand hir the same for to declare.
> Quhat is the cause our boundis bene so bair?
> Quod I: or quhate dois mufe our Miserie?
> Or quhareof dois proceid our povertie?

> For, throw the supporte of your hie prudence,
> Off Scotland I persave the properteis,
> And, als, considderis, be experience,
> Off this countre, the gret commoditeis.
> First, the haboundance of fyschis in our seis,
> And fructual montanis for our bestiall;
> And, for our cornis, mony lusty vaill;

> The ryche Ryveris, plesand and proffitabyll;
> The lustie loochis, with fysche of sindry kyndis;
> Hountyng, halkyng, for nobyllis convenabyll;
> Forrestis ful of Da, Ra, Hartis, and Hyndes;
> The fresche fontanis, quhose holesum cristel strandis
> Refreschis so the fair fluriste grene medis;
> So laik we no thyng that to nature nedis.

> Off every mettel we have the ryche Mynis,
> Baith Gold, Sylver, and stonis precious.
> Howbeit we want the Spyces and the Wynis,
> Or uther strange fructis delycious,

We have als gude, and more neidfull for ws,
Meit, drynk, fyre, clathis, thar mycht be gart abound
Quhilkis als is nocht in al the Mapamound;

More fairer peple, nor of gretar ingyne,
Nor of more strenth gret dedis tyll indure.
Quharefor, I pray yow that ye wald defyne
The principall cause quharefor we ar so pure;
For I marvell gretlie, I yow assure,
Considderand the peple and the ground,
That Ryches suld nocht in this realme redound.

(806–840)

In *The Dreme* and still more in the later *Ane Satyre of the Thrie Estaitis* the transformation of the ragged figure of John the Commonweal is central to Lindsay's purpose. Alexander Scott[71] saw the restoration of the "pure folk" as one of the principal tasks confronting Queen Mary on her return to Scotland in 1561. For a time it looked as if James VI might succeed where his mother and grandfather had failed, and even the events of the middle and later seventeenth century, which turned everything back towards something worse than the *status quo*, did not quench earlier aspirations, and did not radically alter the form which they had taken. The period of the Enlightenment, as it eventually developed, was the consummation of a long process in Scottish life and literature.

NOTES

1. "In Mortem Vicecomitis Taodunensis", A. Pitcairne, *Selecta Poemata* (Edinburgh, 1727), 4. The translation is by J. W. L. Adams, and appears in J. Kinsley (ed.), *Scottish Poetry. A Critical Survey* (London, 1955), 97. In *Selecta Poemata* the epitaph is followed by "Deploratio status Regni Scotici". For Pitcairne, see especially D. Duncan, *Thomas Ruddiman* (Edinburgh and London, 1965), 15–23; W. T. Johnston (ed.), *The Best of Our Owne: Letters of Archibald Pitcairne* (Edinburgh, 1979); F. W. Freeman and A. Law, "Allan Ramsay's first published poem; the poem to the memory of Dr Archibald Pitcairne", *The Bibliotheck* 9 (1979) no 5, 153–160.

2. A. D. Murdoch (ed. and transl.) *The Grameid . . . by James Philip of Almerieclose 1691* (S.H.S., Edinburgh, 1888).

3. John Fordun (c. 1320–c. 1384), *Chronica Gentis Scotorum* III. v.; H. Boece (c. 1465–1536), *Scotorum Historiae* (Paris, 1527), VII. iiii.

4. "Upon the Death of the Viscount of Dundee", J. Sargeaunt (ed.), *The Poems of John Dryden* (Oxford, 1910), 181.

5. Quoted in D. Daiches, *Scotland and the Union* (London, 1977), 161.

6. Sargeaunt, *op. cit.*, 203.

7. "Ane New Yeir Gift to the Quene Mary quhen scho come first hame, 1562", line 31; J. Cranstoun (ed.), *The Poems of Alexander Scott* (S. T. S., Edinburgh and London, 1896), 2.

8. *De Jure Regni apud Scottos* appears in T. Ruddiman (ed.), *Georgii Buchanani Scoti, Poetarum Sui Seculi Facile Principis, Opera Omnia* (2 vols., Edinburgh, 1715), and in most editions of *Rerum Scoticarum Historia*, first published Edinburgh, 1582. See also D. H. MacNeill's translation, *The Art and Science of Government among the Scots* (Glasgow, 1964).

9. D. Craig, *Scottish Literature and the Scottish People* (London, 1961), 152.

10. Murdoch, *op. cit.*, 29–30.

11. Ed. Terence Tobin (Lafayette, Indiana, 1972).

12. Selections are to be found in R. D. S. Jack (ed.), *Scottish Prose 1550–1700* (London, 1971), 192–202.

13. (Edinburgh, 1966). Professor Youngson's book is, of course, a most valuable study of some aspects of Enlightenment culture.

14. See Leslie Shirlaw, "Dr Archibald Pitcairne and Sir Isaac Newton's 'Black Years' (1692–1694)'", *Chronicle of the Royal College of Physicians of Edinburgh* (January, 1975), 23–26. Pitcairne was consulted during the nervous illness which afflicted Newton 1692–1694.

15. W. T. Johnston, *op. cit.*, 38. For Bruno's significance, see especially Frances A. Yates, *Giordano Bruno and the Hermetic Tradition* (London, 1964).

16. W. T. Johnston, *op. cit.*, 19.

17. W. T. Johnston, *op. cit.*, 56–57.

18. *The Wars of Truth* (Cambridge, Mass., 1952), 303–304.

19. Baker, *op. cit.*, 353. Compare the quotation from Reid's Essays on the Intelectual Powers of Man, below pp. 45–46.

20. Baker, *op. cit.*, 321. The reference is to the celebrated *Songe de Descartes*, described by Adrien Baillet (1649–1706) in *La Vie de Monsieur Descartes* (Paris, 1691), 81–86, which in turn is related to the *Poële* episode of *Discours de la methode, deuxieme partie*.

21. For the work of Napier and later mathematicians, see especially R. Schlapp, "The Contribution of the Scots to Mathematics", *Mathematical Gazette* LVII (1973), 1–16. See also Agnes G. Stewart, *The Academic Gregories* (Edinburgh and London, 1901), and entries on individual mathematicians and scientists in DNB.

This may be the place to mention the peculiar contribution of Sir Thomas Urquhart (1611–1660) to mathematics. Urquhart is best known for his translation of Rabelais (1653), for the account of the Admirable Crichton, which appears in *The Discovery of a most Exquisite Jewel* (1652), and for his scheme of a universal language, referred to in the *Jewel* and in *Logopandecteision* (1653). One aspect at least of his universal language is probably to be seen in *The Trissotetras* (1645), a treatise on trigonometry written in a purpose-built artificial vocabulary, and in terms of the Art of Memory as understood by the Middle Ages and Renaissance. "Now, if to those helps for the memorie which in this table I have afforded the reader, both by the alphabetical order of some consonants, and homogeneity of others in their affections of sharpnesse, meannesse, obtusity, and duplicity, be joyne that artificiall aid in having every part of the schemes locally in his mind, of all wayes, both for facility in remembring, and stedfastnesse of retention, without doubt the most expedite, or otherwise place the representatives of words, according to the method of the art of memory in the severall corners of a house, which, in regard of their paucity, are containable within a parlour and dining roome at most, he may, with ease, get them all by heart in lesse than the space of an houre, which is no great expence of time, though bestowed on matters of meaner consequence" (*The Works of Sir Thomas Urquhart of Cromarty, Knight*, Maitland Club 30, Edinburgh, 1834, 78). On the relation between ideas of a universal language and the Art of Memory, see Paoli Rossi, *Clavis Universalis* (Milan-Naples, 1960, chapter VII, and note how Frances A. Yates (*The Art of Memory*, London, 1966, 364, 368) follows Rossi in connecting it with the seventeenth century refinement of scientific method, as exemplified particularly by the work of Leibnitz (1646–1716). See also J. Derrick McClure, "The 'Universal Languages' of Thomas Urquhart and George Dalgarno", *Actes du 2ᵉ colloque de lanque et de litterature ecossaises (moyen age et renaissance)* (Strasbourg, 1979), 133–147.

22. Schlapp, *op. cit.*
23. Quotations are from *Georgii Buchanani Scoti Poemata in Tres Partes Digesta* (London, 1686). *De Sphaera* occupies pp. 468–540. See also J. R. Naiden's translation (n.p., 1952). *De Sphaera* was originally addressed to the son of Buchanan's patron, the Maréchal de Brissac, but was continued after Buchanan's return to Scotland about 1561. Left incomplete at his death, it was brought to a conclusion by Adam King (?1560–1620).

I have occasionally corrected obvious misprints in the Latin text.

A stimulating account of European astronomical developments in the sixteenth and seventeenth centuries is to be found in A. Koestler, *The Sleepwalkers* (London, 1959).

24. A. J. Meadows, *The High Firmament. A Survey of Astronomy in English Literature* (Leicester, 1969), 73.
25. "A Description of the Intellectual Globe", J. M. Robertson (ed.), *The Philosophical Works of Francis Bacon* (London, 1905), 685.
26. J. Craigie (ed.), *The Poems of James VI of Scotland*, II (S.T.S., Edinburgh and London, 1958), 101.
27. H. Diels and W. Kranz, *Die Fragmente der Vorsokratiker* (6th ed., 3 vols., Berlin, 1951–1952), 44A21, quoted and translated by W. K. C. Guthrie, *A History of Greek Philosophy I The Earlier Presocratics and the Pythagoreans* (Cambridge, 1962), 284.
28. *Metaphysics* 986a3, quoted and translated by Guthrie, *op. cit.*, 287–288.
29. J. C. Polkinghorne, *The Particle Play* (Oxford, 1979), 60–61.
30. Frances A. Yates, *op. cit.*, 153–154.
31. "At the centre of everything the sun has his seat. For in this most beautiful temple, who might put this luminary in a place other or better than one from which it may simultaneously be able to enlighten the whole? In truth, not inappropriately do some call it the lamp, others the mind, others the ruler, of the universe. Trismegistus calls it the visible god."
32. R. H. MacDonald (ed.), *William Drummond of Hawthornden. Poems and Prose* (A.S.L.S., Edinburgh and London, 1976). *Flowres of Sion* occupies pp. 88–128; *Poems: The First Part* and *The Second Part*, pp. 8–72. A good recent study, not mentioned by Dr MacDonald is E. Paganelli, *La Poesia di Drummond of Hawthornden* (Bari, 1972).

33. On the text from *Wisdom of Solomon*, see especially E. R. Curtius, *European Literature and the Latin Middle Ages* (tr. by Willard R. Trask, London, 1953), Excursus XV, "Numerical Composition", 501–509. The text is quoted by Henryson, "Preiching of the Swallow", 53, a poem which has a numerological basis in some ways resembling that of "An Hymne of the Fairest Faire".

34. On Henryson's Platonism, see especially my "Neoplatonism and Orphism in Fifteenth-Century Scotland. The Evidence of Henryson's *New Orpheus*", *Scottish Studies* 20 (1976), 69–89.

35. Koestler, *op. cit.*, 317ff.

36. Koestler, *op. cit.*, 353.

37. See especially Meadows, *op. cit.*, chapter IV, "The Copernican Revolution".

38. "An Anatomy of the World. The first Anniversary", lines 205ff., Sir Herbert Grierson (ed.), *The Poems of John Donne* (London, 1933), 213.

39. MacDonald, *op. cit.*, 154.

40. The line contains a half-disguised reference to Cicero's Platonic *Somnium Scipionis*, chapter V. "Consider the people who dwell in the region about the Great Cataract, where the Nile comes rushing down from lofty mountains; they have lost their sense of hearing because of the loud roar. But the sound coming from the heavenly spheres revolving at very swift speeds is of course so great that human ears cannot catch it; you might as well try to stare directly at the sun, whose rays are much too strong for your eyes" (W. H. Stahl, transl., *Macrobius. Commentary on the Dream of Scipio*, New York and London, 1952, 74). It should be noted that Drummond's lines contain no specific reference to moving spheres.

41. "Preiching of the Swallow", *The Morall Fabillis of Esope the Phrygian*, C. Elliott (ed.), *Robert Henryson. Poems* (Oxford, 1963), 50.

42. Frances A. Yates, *op. cit.*, 152.

43. Ibid.

44. Above, p.17

45. In 1613 Drummond wrote to a certain M. W. K., a kinsman of Buchanan: "A more learned man than your Cousin was this country has not brought forth; and now we see, by the incommodities of this country, his excellent works, especially his *Sphaera*, appear not to the world. Many noble pieces of our countrymen are drowned in oblivion *per σκοτιαν Scotorum*". D. Masson, *Drummond of Hawthornden* (London, 1873), 34–35.

46. Koestler, *op. cit.*, 46–50. See also T. L. Heath, *Aristarchus of Samos* (Oxford, 1913), 249; E. Frank, *Plato und die sogenannten Pythagoreer* (Halle, 1923) 209ff.

47. Made public in the second volume of the posthumous *Astronomiae instauratae progymnasmata* (Prague, 1602–1603), edited by Kepler. The second volume is the *De mundi aetherei recentioribus phaenomenis*, mentioned above p. 13.

48. *The History of Scotland* (London 1645), 212; "A Speech on Toleration", MacDonald, *op. cit.*, 175–176.

49. L. E. Kastner (ed.), *The Poetical Works of William Drummond of Hawthornden* (2 vols., S.T.S., London and Edinburgh, 1913), II. 228.

50. MacDonald, *op. cit.*, 136–139.

51. *The Entertainement of the High and Mighty Monarch, Prince Charles, King of Great Brittaine, France and Ireland, into his Ancient and Royall Citie of Edenbourgh, the 15 of Iune 1633*, Kastner, *op. cit.*, II. 113–136.

52. Kastner, *op. cit.*, II. 117–118.

53. Kastner, *op. cit.*, II. 243.

54. *Forth Feasting. A Panegyricke to the Kings Most Excellent Majesty*, Kastner, *op. cit.*, I. 141–153.
55. Kastner, *op. cit.*, II. 192.
56. D. Masson, *Drummond of Hawthornden* (London, 1873), 443.
57. For the academic Gregories, see footnote 21 above.
58. Sir William Geddes and W. K. Leask (eds.), *Musa Latina Aberdonensis* (3 vols., New Spalding Club, Aberdeen, 1892, 1895, 1910), II. 21. The translation is by J. W. L. Adams, and appears in J. Kinsley (ed.), *op. cit.*, 91.
59. See especially H. R. Fletcher, W. H. Brown, *The Royal Botanic Garden Edinburgh 1670–1970* (Edinburgh, 1970), and articles on individual botanists in D.N.B.
60. Extracts are to be found in R. D. S. Jack (ed.), *Scottish Prose 1550–1700* (London, 1971), 154–172.
61. Most recently edited by Stewart Sanderson, *The Secret Common-Wealth & A Short Treatise of Charms and Spels by Robert Kirk* (Folklore Society, Mistletoe Series, Cambridge, 1976).
62. In his edition of *The Secret Commonwealth* (1893; reprinted Stirling, 1933), 21.
63. See J. I. Cope and H. W. Jones (eds.), *History of the Royal Society by Thomas Sprat* (St Louis, 1958). The full title of Sprat's work, which appeared in 1667, is *The History of the Institution, Design and Progress of the Royal Society of London for the Advancement of Experimental Philosophy*.
64. See especially J. I. Cope, *Joseph Glanvill Anglican Apologist* (St Louis, 1956). For the general situation in England, see especially K. Thomas, *Religion and the Decline of Magic* (London, 1971; Peregrine editn., London, 1978).
65. Sanderson, *op. cit.*, 62.
66. Sanderson, *op. cit.*, 49–51.
67. "Preiching of the Swallow", Elliott, *op. cit.*, 50.
68. Carl L. Becker, *The Heavenly City of the Eighteenth Century Philosophers* (New Haven, 1932; reprinted 1971).
69. *Ballattis of Luve* (Edinburgh, 1970), liii–lix.
70. D. Hamer (ed.), *The Works of Sir David Lindsay of the Mount 1490–1555*, I (S.T.S., Edinburgh and London, 1931), 28–29.
71. "Pure folk ar famist with thir fassionis new", "Ane New Yeir Gift to the Quene Mary quhen scho come first hame, 1562", line 137. (Above, footnote 7.)

CHAPTER II

THE NATURAL PHILOSOPHY OF MAN: Hume, Reid and Montesquieu

In the long run, the most influential book written by a Scot of the earlier Enlightenment was probably David Hume's *A Treatise of Human Nature*. Hume (1711–1776) is better known as a philosopher than as a practical or literary man, yet a strikingly small part, even of the *Treatise*, is devoted to abstract philosophy. The sub-title – "An Attempt to Introduce the Experimental Method of Reasoning into Moral Subjects" – indicates the practical and scientific bias of his investigations. Hume from the beginning of his work placed himself squarely in the tradition of Bacon's *Novum Organum*[1]:—

> "And as the science of man is the only solid foundation for the other sciences, so the only solid foundation we can give to this science itself must be laid on experience and observation. 'Tis no astonishing reflection to consider, that the application of experimental philosophy to moral subjects should come after that to natural at the distance of above a whole century; since we find in fact, that there was about the same interval betwixt the origins of these sciences; and that reckoning from Thales to Socrates, the space of time is nearly equal to that betwixt my Lord Bacon and some late philosophers in *England*, who have begun to put the science of man on a new footing, and have engaged the attention and excited the curiosity of the public. So true it is, that however other nations may rival us in poetry, and excel us in some other agreeable arts, the improvement in reason and philosophy can only be owing to a land of toleration and liberty."

As the development of the *Treatise* indicates, moral subjects for Hume were essentially matters of methodical psychological investigation. His great contemporary and opponent, (Aquinas, as it were, to his Occam) Thomas Reid (1710–1796), however different his conclusions, proposed the same object, the same history for, and methodical approach to, his subject. I quote from the preface to *Essays on the Intellectual Powers of Man*[2]:—

> "About two hundred years ago, the opinions of men in natural philosophy were as various and contradictory as they are now concerning the powers of the mind. Galileo, Torricelli, Kepler, Bacon and Newton, had the same discouragement in their attempts to throw light upon the material system, as we have with regard to the intellectual. If they had been deterred by such prejudices, we should never have reaped the benefit of their discoveries, which do honour to human nature, and will make their names immortal. The motto which Lord Bacon prefixed to some of his writing was worthy of his genius, *Inveniam viam aut faciam*.
>
> There is a natural order in the progress of the sciences, and good reasons may be assigned why the philosophy of body should be *elder sister* to that of mind, and of a quicker growth; but the last hath the principle of life no less than the first and will grow up, though slowly, to maturity. The remains of ancient philosophy upon this subject, are venerable ruins, carrying the marks of genius and industry, sufficient to inflame but not to satisfy our curiosity. In later ages, Des Cartes was the first that pointed out the road we ought to take in those dark regions. Malebranche, Arnauld, Locke, Berkeley, Buffier, Hutcheson, Butler, Hume, Price, Lord Kames, have laboured to make discoveries – nor have they laboured in vain; for, however different and contrary their conclusions are, however sceptical some of them, they have all given new light, and cleared the way to those who shall come after them.
>
> We ought never to despair of human genius, but rather to hope that, in time, it may produce a system of the powers and operations of the human mind, no less certain than those of optics or astronomy."

The memorial tablet to Reid in Glasgow University assumes a parallel between the achievement of Bacon in the establishment of physical science, the *Instauratio Magna*, and that of Reid, *qui, in scientia mentis humanae, ut olim in philosophia naturali illustris ille Baconus Verulaminus, omnia instauravit*. Reid's insistence that the basis of any mental philosophy must be Common Sense implied that the methodology appropriate to the subject was identical with that of the physical sciences.

Hume and Reid alike were Baconians who regarded themselves as midwives for the birth of a new science. Both were also much impressed by the work of Newton – Hume, indeed, saw in the Association of Ideas a principle as generally and fruitfully applicable as the Law of Gravitation[3]. "These are therefore the principles of union or cohesion among our simple ideas, and in the imagination supply the place of that inseparable annexion, by which they are united in our memory. Here is a kind of ATTRACTION, which in the mental world will be found to have as extraordinary effects as in the natural, and to shew itself in as many and as various forms."

In *An Abstract of a Book lately Published; Entituled, A Treatise of Human Nature &c.*[4] (1740), he gave a brief indication of the implications, as he saw them:—

> " 'Twill be easy to conceive of what vast consequences these principles must be in the science of human nature, if we consider, that so far as regards the mind, these are the only links that bind the parts of the universe together, or connect us with any person or object exterior to ourselves. For as it is by means of thought only that anything operates upon our passions, and as these are the only ties of our thoughts, they are really *to us* the cement of the universe, and all the operations of the mind must, in a great measure, depend on them."

(The principles mentioned are resemblance, continuity, and causation, the three constituents of the Association of Ideas.) Hume's assessment of Newton's total achievement is to be found in the *History of England*[5]:—

> "In Newton this island may boast of having produced the greatest and rarest genius that ever rose for the ornament and instruction of the species. Cautious in admitting no principles but such as were founded on experiment; but resolute to adopt every such principle, however new or unusual; from modesty, ignorant of his superiority above the rest of mankind, and thence, less careful to accommodate his reasonings to common apprehensions; more anxious to merit than acquire fame; he was, from these causes, long unknown to the world; but his reputation at last broke out with a lustre which scarcely any writer, during his own life-time, had ever before attained. While Newton seemed to draw off the veil from some of the mysteries of nature, he showed at the same time the imperfections of the mechanical philosophy, and thereby restored her ultimate secrets to that obscurity, in which they ever did and ever will remain."

Professor Mossner has commented[6] that the sceptical and positivistic aspects of the Newtonian methodology appealed strongly to Hume and were taken over by him as well as the experimental "Like the poet Donne a century earlier, Hume was convinced that 'new Philosophy calls all in doubt'". (In this, it will be remembered, he resembles Drummond as well as Donne.) It may be added that Hume saw in Newton's career one which to a considerable extent ran parallel with his own.

Reid, who on his mother's side was one of the academic Gregories, and at Marischal College, Aberdeen, had been a pupil of the mathematician and expositor of Newton, Colin McLaurin (1698–1746) is even more explicitly a Newtonian than Hume: indeed, his main objection to Hume, as to other distinguished philosophers, is that they are not sufficiently Newtonian. Like Hume, he admired Newton's caution; for him *Hypotheses non fingo* is the central statement of Newton's philosophical method, a statement ignored by others at their peril[7]:—

"Let us, therefore, lay down this as a fundamental principle in our inquiries into the structure of the mind and its operations – that no regard is due to the conjectures or hypotheses of philosophers, however ancient, however generally received. Let us accustom ourselves to try every opinion by the touchstone of fact and experience. What can fairly be deduced from facts duly observed or sufficiently attested, is genuine and pure; it is the voice of God, and no fiction of human imagination.

The first rule of philosophising laid down by the great Newton, is this:— *Causas rerum naturalium, non plures admitti debere, quam quae et verae sint, et earum phaenomenis explicandis sufficiant.* 'No more causes, nor any other causes of natural effects, ought to be admitted, but such as are both true, and are sufficient for explaining their appearances.' This is a golden rule; it is the true and proper test, by which what is sound and solid in philosophy may be distinguished from what is hollow and vain.

If the philosopher, therefore, pretends to shew us the cause of any natural effect, whether relating to matter or to mind, let us first consider whether there is sufficient evidence that the cause he assigns does really exist. If there is not, reject it with disdain, as a fiction which ought to have no place in genuine philosophy. If the cause assigned really exists, consider, in the next place, whether the effect it is brought to explain necessarily follows from it. Unless it has these two conditions, it is good for nothing.

When Newton had shewn the admirable effects of gravitation in our planetary system, he must have felt a strong desire to know its cause. He could have invented a hypothesis for this purpose as many had done before him. But his philosophy was of another complexion. Let us hear what he says: *Rationem harum gravitatis proprietatum ex phaenomenis non potui deducere, et hypotheses non fingo. Quicquid enim ex phaenomenis non deducitur, hypothesis vocanda est. Et hypotheses, seu metaphysicae, seu physicae, seu qualitatum occultarum, seu mechanicae, in philosophia experimentali locum non habent.*"

Hume, he suggests — and, however extensive the consequences, this is virtually the one basic point of difference between them — built the entire structure of his philosophy on an unsupported hypothesis, the status of which he leaves undefined[8]:—

"What other authors, from the time of Des Cartes, had called *ideas*, this author" (Hume, that is to say) "distinguishes into two kinds — to wit, *impressions* and *ideas*; comprehending under the first, all our sensations, passions, and emotions; and under the last, the faint images of these, when we remember or imagine them.

He sets out with this, as a principle that needed no proof, and of which therefore he offers none — that all the perceptions of the human mind resolve themselves into these two kinds, *impressions* and *ideas*.

As this proposition is the foundation upon which the whole of Mr Hume's system rests, and from which it is raised with great acuteness indeed, and ingenuity, it were to be wished that he had told us upon what authority this fundamental proposition rests. But we are left to guess, whether it is held forth as a first principle, which has its evidence in itself; or whether it is to be received upon the authority of philosophers."

More positively, in Essay I.II[9], Reid notes that Newton set a model "by laying down the common principles or axioms, on which the reasonings in natural philosophy are based". As a consequence, in his own Essay VI, *Of Judgment*, V and VI, he was careful to list the First Principles of Contingent Truths, and the First Principles of Necessary Truths, on which the Newtonian structure of the Common Sense philosophy is raised.

Nothing in all this implies that either Reid or Hume adopted a materialistic approach to the mind. There is no Scottish equivalent of La Mettrie's *L'Homme machine* (1748) or of Holbach's *Système de la nature* (1770). The mental and moral sciences had the same autonomy as the natural, and of necessity therefore differed in the object of investigation. The task of the philosopher was to systematize and relate the multifarious phenomena of the human mind. *A Treatise of Human Nature* is divided into three books, dealing respectively with the Understanding, the Passions, and Morals: the result is a human psychology, based on the central paradox[10] that "Reason is, and ought only to be, the slave of the passions".

Reid's first major work was the *Enquiry into the Human Mind* (1764), and all his later works are in some sense psychological. Both philosophers are concerned with the oddities, as well as the regularities, of the human mind. Their work finds many parallels, conscious and unconscious, in the work of the Scottish novelists of the next century. "Curious anomalous facts in the history of mind"[11], as given shape, for instance, by the differing behaviour of the sisters Jeannie and Effie Deans in *The Heart of Midlothian* or by the developing character of Henry Morton in *Old Mortality*, became the staple of Scott's best fiction, and the John Galt who wrote *The Provost*, *The Entail* and *The Member* knew his Hume and Reid as well as his Machiavelli. Much of the second volume of this book will be given over to the novelists, and as they themselves also realized, the operations of the mind extend beyond the individual into history, political economy and sociology (to name no others), all of which are based on the individual, but whose confines are less limited to the individual than are those of psychology.

ii

Hume himself was prepared to use his method in other fields, most notably in that of history. The inductive, experimental method is as clearly present in such a passage as this from *The History of Great Britain* as in anything from the *Treatise*. Hume is dealing with the reign of James VI and I[12]:—

"The price of corn, during this reign, and by consequence, that of the other necessaries of life, was no lower, or was rather higher, than at present. By a proclamation of James, establishing public magazines, whenever wheat fell below thirty two shillings a quarter, rye below eighteen, barley below sixteen, the commissioners were empowered to purchase corn for the magazines. These prices then are to be regarded as low;

tho' they would pass for very high by our present estimation. The best wool, during the greatest part of James's reign, was at thirty three shillings a tod: At present, it is not above two thirds of that value; tho' it is to be presumed, that our exports in woolen goods are considerably increased. The finer manufactures too, by the progress of art and industry, have been kept pretty near at the same value, if they have not rather diminished, notwithstanding the great increase of money. In Shakespear, the hostess tells Falstaff, that the shirts she bought him were holland at eight shillings a yard; a very high price at this day, even supposing, what is not probable, that the best holland at that time was equal in goodness to the best which can now be purchased. In like manner, a yard of velvet, about the middle of Elizabeth's reign, was valued at two and twenty shillings. I have not been able by any inquiry to learn the common price of butcher meat during the reign of James: But as bread is the chief article of food, and its price regulates that of everything else, we may presume, that cattle bore a high value as well as corn. Besides, we must consider, that the general turn of that age, which no laws could prevent, was the converting arable into pasture: A certain proof that the latter was found more profitable, and consequently that all butcher meat, as well as bread, was considerably higher than at present. We have a regulation of the market with regard to poultry and some other articles, very early in Charles reign; and the prices are high. A turkey cock four shillings and sixpence, a turkey hen three shillings, a pheasant cock six shillings, a pheasant hen five shillings, a partridge one shilling, a goose two shillings, a capon two and sixpence, a pullet one and sixpence, a rabbit eight pence, a dozen of pigeons six shillings. We must consider, that London at present is more than three times the bulk it was at that time. A circumstance, which much increases the price of poultry and of every thing that cannot conveniently be brought from a distance. The chief difference in expence betwixt that age and the present consists in the imaginary wants of men, which have since extremely multiplied. These are the principal reasons, why James's revenue would go farther than the same money in our time; tho' the difference is not so great as is usually imagined.''

   This passage owes much to the emphasis on humble economic fact at the expense of the dignity of history, an emphasis which in turn results, at least partially, from the application of the direct experimental method to historical investigation. Hume certainly owes something of this to another Newtonian, Voltaire, whose *Siècle de Louis XIV* appeared in 1751 and whose *Essai sur les moeurs et l'esprit des nations* reached its final public shape in 1769. It must be added that he was also influenced by a distinctively Scottish historical tradition and style of presentation – the work, that is to say, of his somewhat less enlightened predecessors, for example, the *History of the Reformation in Scotland* by John Knox (1505–1572), the *History of the Church and State in Scotland* by John Spottiswoode (1565–1639), Archbishop of St Andrews, the *History of the Reformation of the Church of England* and *History of His Own Time* by Gilbert Burnet (1643–1715), the Glasgow divinity professor who eventually became Bishop of Salisbury, and whose historical writings provoked the wrath of Bossuet (1627–1704) in *Histoire des variations des églises protestantes*. (Voltaire and Hume alike reacted against the emphasis on divine providence in Bossuet's *Discours sur l'histoire universelle*.) Hume's central interest as an enlightened historian lay in the Reformation and the civil wars which followed, the period which saw the birth of modern times, as he would have understood the term. It was for this very period that the earlier Scottish historians had produced their best and most vivid work. They tended however to concentrate on events of which their knowledge was at first, or a close second, hand, and this gave their writing a factual immediacy parallel to that which Hume, here and elsewhere, achieved by different methods and for a different purpose. The contrast between the ideas and assumptions of his own time and those familiar to his predecessors, was powerfully illustrated by the incidental personal material in their books, and helped to develop in Hume his notable sense of period and social and intellectual change. Burnet, indeed, had already, if only crudely and half-consciously, achieved something of the same kind[13]:—

> "In the third year of his (Charles I's) reign the earl of
> Nithisdale, then believed a papist, which he afterwards
> professed, having married a niece of the duke of Buckingham's,
> was sent down with a power to take the surrender of all church
> lands, and to assure all who did readily surrender, that the king
> would take it kindly, and use them all very well, but that he
> would proceed with all rigour against those who would not
> submit their rights to his disposal. Upon his coming down,
> those who were most concerned in those grants met at
> Edinburgh, and agreed, that when they were called together, if
> no other argument did prevail to make the earl of Nithisdale

desist, they would fall upon him and all his party in the old Scottish manner, and knock them on the head. Primrose told me one of these lords, Belhaven of the name of Douglas, who was blind, bid them set him by one of the party, and he would make sure of one. So he was set next the earl of Dumfries: he was all the while holding him fast: and when the other asked him what he meant by that, he said, ever since the blindness was come on him he was in such fear of falling, that he could not help holding fast to those who were next to him: he had all the while a poniard in his other hand, with which he had certainly stabbed Dumfries if any disturbance had happened. The appearance at that time was so great, and so much heat was raised upon it, that the earl of Nithisdale would not open all his instructions, but came back to court, looking on the service as desperate: so a stop was put to it for some time.''

Burnet was aware of the gap separating himself and his readers from "the old Scottish manner". Hume saw more of the intellectual possibilities inherent in such contrasts, and insights of the type which he thus obtained were afterwards exploited to the imaginative full by Walter Scott and John Galt.

The greatest Scottish political economist was Adam Smith (1723–1790), but Hume also wrote on the subject – indeed, there is a good deal of implicit political economy in the passage just quoted. As a sociologist, he achieved nothing significant, but abroad a method resembling his own was applied to sociology by his elder contemporary Montesquieu (1689–1755), most notably in the *Esprit des Lois*. This is perhaps more important for the development of the Scottish Enlightenment than even the *Treatise*; it was translated and often reprinted in Scotland[14]: it helped to solve a recurrent Scottish dilemma, which Hume himself may serve to exemplify. In the *History* his references to Scotland are generally slighting, even contemptuous[15]. "Never did refined Athens so exult in diffusing the sciences and liberal arts over the savage world: Never did generous Rome so please herself in the view of law and order established by her victorious arms: As the Scotch now rejoiced, in communicating their barbarous zeal, and theological fervor, to the neighbouring nations." Elsewhere, he uses similar terms to describe the success of the Scottish preachers in London[16]. "All the eloquence of parliament, now well refined from pedantry, animated with the spirit of liberty, and employed in such important interests, was not attended to with such insatiable avidity, as were these lectures, delivered with ridiculous cant, and a provincial accent, full of barbarism and of ignorance."

"Provincial" is the important word. It was easy for eighteenth century Scots, unaware of, or unsympathetic to, the national achievements of the Middle Ages and the Renaissance, but acutely conscious of the difference in status, affluence and churchmanship between Scotland and England, to despise their inheritance and circumstances. The confidence which in the fifteenth century had enabled Henryson to make easy heraldic jests about English subordination to Scotland had almost completely disappeared. The loss of formal national status contributed to this, but also involved was a loss of faith in what previously had been the accepted history of Scotland. "We are only a small kingdom, but for two thousand years we have stood free of any foreign yoke: from our earliest days we have created lawful kings", said Buchanan in *De Iure Regni apud Scottos*[17] with a confidence echoed more than a hundred years later by Philip in the *Grameid* when he condemns (in a way which certainly would have surprised Buchanan) the usurpation of royal power by William II[18]. The accepted scheme of Scottish history was ultimately based on the work of early Christian Irish scholars who distorted their own traditions to establish a place for their nation in the Eusebius/ Jerome/Prosper tables of universal history, and this in turn had been elaborated, and further distorted, in the works of John of Fordun (*c.* 1320–*c.* 1384), Walter Bower (*c.* 1385–1449), Hector Boece (*c.* 1465–1536), and Buchanan himself[19]. The essential purpose of the developed scheme was to vindicate Scottish rights and conduct against English claims and continental hostility and so to maintain national confidence; the demolition, at least of the first forty kings, and the rehabilitation of the Picts and Britons by Father Thomas Innes (1662–1744) in *A Critical Essay on the Ancient Inhabitants of the Northern Parts of Britain or Scotland* (1729) marks a development in historical scholarship, in absolute terms as important as Richard Bentley's demolition of the *Epistles of Phalaris* (1699), and of much greater significance in terms of its effect on national morale. It facilitated scepticism about the entire early history of Scotland, and indeed made the claim of a separate history and culture seem dubious to many. Others over-compensated for their loss. The gigantic Ossianic world-scheme, and the pseudo-history which sometimes enfeebles the poetry of Robert Fergusson, are direct consequences of Innes's *Essay* – outposts or redoubts in a Scottish Battle of the Books.

From all this, the *Esprit des Lois* was the great liberator. Montesquieu treated variations in cultures and traditions as the products of impersonal environment, with no necessary implication of superiority or inferiority. The titles of the individual Books demonstrate his scientific approach[20]; "Of laws as relative to the nature of the climate" (XIV): "Of laws in the relation they bear to the nature of the soil" (XVIII): "Of laws in relation to the principles which form the general spirit, the morals and customs of a nation" (XIX). All this and much more has an obvious relationship to the otherwise apparently unique Scottish experience, which the scientific and imaginative insight of Montesquieu set in a context the reverse of provincial oddity. Montesquieu is substantially responsible for the fact that Scottish fiction (and to some extent Scottish poetry also) is so much concerned with "manners"; "manners" however in Montesquieu's sense, and with the implications of Montesquieu's method, rather than the later, more pejorative sense attributed to the word, for instance by Dr Craig in his *Scottish Literature and the Scottish People*[21]. The Scot's image of his nation and himself, as presented in later literature, might almost be based on a cento from *Esprit des Lois*:—

> "From this delicacy of organs peculiar to warm climates, it follows, that the soul is most sensibly moved by whatever has a relation to the union of the two sexes: here everything leads to this object. In northern climates scarce has the animal part of love a power of making itself felt . . . In northern countries, we meet with a people who have few vices, many virtues, a great share of frankness and sincerity . . . In temperate climates we find the inhabitants inconstant in their manners, in their very vices, and in their virtues: the climate has not a quality determinate enough to fix them."

> (XIV.ii.)

> "In mountainous countries, as they have but little, they may preserve what they have. The liberty they enjoy, or, in other words, the government they are under, is the only blessing worthy of their defence. It reigns therefore more in mountainous and difficult countries, than in those which nature seems to have most favoured.
> The mountaineers preserve a more moderate government; because they are not so liable to be conquered."
> "Countries are not cultivated in proportion to their fertility, but to their liberty."

> (XVIII.ii–iii.)

> "Vanity is as advantageous to a government, as pride is dangerous. To be convinced of this, we need only represent, on the one hand, the numberless benefits which result from vanity;

from thence arises luxury, industry, arts, fashion, politeness,
taste: and, on the other, the infinite evils which spring from the
pride of certain nations, laziness, poverty, an universal
neglect."

(XIX.ix.)

"Commerce is a cure for the most destructive prejudices; for
it is almost a general rule, that where we find agreeable
manners, there commerce flourishes; and that where ever there
is commerce, there we meet with agreeable manners. Let us not
be astonished then, if our manners are now less savage than
formerly."

(XX.i.)

"The spirit of trade produces in the mind of man a certain
sense of exact justice, opposite on the one hand to robbery, and
on the other to those moral virtues which forbid our always
adhering rigidly to our own private interest, and suffer us to
neglect it for the advantage of others."

(XX.ii.)

"By the nature of the human understanding, we love in
religion every thing which carries the idea of difficulty; as in
point of morality we have a speculative fondness for every
thing which bears the character of severity."

(XXV.iv.)

"It is a principle, that every religion which is persecuted,
becomes itself persecuting: for as soon as by some accidental
turn it arises from persecution, it attacks the religion which
persecuted it; not as a religion, but as a tyranny."

(XXV.ix.)

The same tendency towards practicality, towards the scientific method,
is visible in Montesquieu as in Hume, and it is in this respect that the
Treatise and *Esprit des Lois* should be compared with the work of the later
Scots, which they clearly influenced; Adam Ferguson, for instance,, and
his *An Essay on the History of Civil Society* (1767), Adam Smith and *An
Inquiry into the Nature and Causes of the Wealth of Nations* (1776), even Lord
Kames and *The Gentleman Farmer, being an attempt to improve Agriculture by
subjecting it to the Test of Rational Principles* (1776). This last indeed is
closest of all to the central practical achievements of this period. Each of
the works particularly emphasises the experimental method, the most
obvious triumphs of which were eventually to be seen in the improved
farmlands of lowland Scotland, in James Watt's steam engine, and in the
mercantile and industrial development of the Clyde-Forth valley. In

Scotland, the Enlightenment meant,in the first place, an increase in the comfort and prosperity of urban and rural life, certainly for the middle and upper classes, to a considerable degree also for the luckier, and the more intelligent, members of the working classes. In the flush of immediate achievement, the incidental creation of urban and rural squalor at home, of poverty and oppression abroad, tended to be over-looked, or at least minimized in importance.

NOTES

1. E. C. Mossner (ed.), *A Treatise of Human Nature* (London, 1969), 43–44.
2. Sir William Hamilton (ed.), *Reid's Essays on the Intellectual Powers of Man* (Edinburgh and London, 1853), 217.
3. *A Treatise of Human Nature* I.i.iv; Mossner, *op. cit.*, 60.
4. Quoted in E. C. Mossner, *The Life of David Hume* (Oxford, 1954), 127.
5. Hume, *History of England* (Edinburgh, 1792), viii, 334.
6. *The Life of David Hume*, 75.
7. Hamilton, *op. cit.*, 236.
8. Hamilton, *op. cit.*, 292–293.
9. Hamilton, *op. cit.*, 231.
10. *A Treatise of Human Nature* II.iii.iii., Mossner's edition, 462.
11. The phrase is used by the advocate Hardie in the first chapter of *The Heart of Midlothian*.
12. D. Forbes (ed.), *Hume. The History of Great Britain. The Reigns of James I and Charles I* (London, 1970), 234–235.
13. *Bishop Burnet's History of His Own Time* (6 vols., Oxford, 1823), I.34–35.
14. Alison K. Howard, "Montesquieu, Voltaire and Rousseau in eighteenth century Scotland", *The Bibliotheck* 2–3 (1959–1962), 40–63. For a general study of Montesquieu see especially R. Shackleton, *Montesquieu A Critical Biography* (Oxford, 1961).
15. Forbes, *op. cit.*, 449.
16. Forbes, *op. cit.*, 413–414.
17. (Edinburgh, 1579), 102. *Nos regnum exiguum quidem, sed iam bis mille annos ab exterarum gentium imperio liberum tenemus. Reges legitimos ab initio creavimus.* The translation is by MacNeill (above, Chapter 1 footnote 8).
18. Murdoch, *op. cit.*, 29–30.
19. See Chapter I, footnotes 3 and 8 above. Walter Bower's *Scotichronicon* was completed by 1449, the year of his death.
20. I have used an anonymous eighteenth century translation, *The Spirit of Laws* (Third Edition, 2 vols., Edinburgh, 1762).
21. Craig, *op. cit.*, 151ff.

CHAPTER III

LITERATURE, SCIENCE AND IMPROVEMENT: Ramsay, Thomson and Smollett

All the factors mentioned in earlier sections are found combined in the general literature of the period. Allan Ramsay (1684–1758), for instance, in one fairly typical poem, "The Prospect of Plenty"[1], is the prophet of commercial success and urban and rural improvement – a John the Baptist of the Agricultural and Industrial revolutions:—

> Plenty shall cultivate ilk Scawp and Moor,
> Now Lee and bare, because the Landlord's poor.
> On scroggy Braes shall Akes and Ashes grow,
> And bonny Gardens clead the brecken How.
> Does others backward dam the raging Main,
> Raising on barren Sands a flowry Plain?
> By us then shou'd the Thought o't be endur'd
> To let braid Tracts of Land ly unmanur'd?
> Uncultivate nae mair they shall appear,
> But shine with a' the Beauties of the Year;
> Which start with Ease frae the obedient Soil,
> And ten Times o'er reward a little Toil.
>
> Alang wild shore, where tumbling Billows break,
> Plenisht with nought but Shells and Tangle-Wreck,
> Braw Towns shall rise, with Steeples mony a ane,
> And Houses bigget a' with Estler Stane:
> Where Schools polite shall lib'ral Arts display,
> And make auld barb'rous Darkness fly away.
>
> (215–232)

(The adverse comparison of Scotland with the Low Countries, where so many young Scots completed their education, is not to be missed.) Nor is it accidental that in another poem, written after the death of Newton in

1727 and dedicated to the Royal Society, Ramsay (like many others)
celebrated the achievement of the great *savant*[2]:—

> The God-like *Man* now mounts the Sky,
> Exploring all yon radiant Spheres;
> And with one View can more descry,
> Than here below in eighty Years.
>
> Tho' none, with greater Strength of Soul,
> Could rise to more divine a Height.
> Or range the *Orbs* from *Pole* to *Pole*,
> And more improve the humane Sight.
>
> Now with full Joy he can survey
> These Worlds, and every shining Blaze,
> That countless in the *Milky Way*,
> Only thro' Glasses shew their Rays.
>
> (5–16)

Newton, by the theoretical and practical application of scientific
principles, had brought a richer universe within reach of human
knowledge. By a corresponding application of scientific principles, it
was now possible for the Scots to make a wilderness civilized.

A similar viewpoint is to be found in another poet of the period, James
Thomson (1700–1748), who left the University of Edinburgh for
London in 1724, and published *Winter*, which was afterwards enlarged
to become *The Seasons*, in 1726. The first version of *Winter* was not particularly Newtonian, but as Marjorie Nicolson[3] in particular has
established, Thomson soon became pre-eminently the poet of the
Newtonian synthesis. In "To the Memory of Sir Isaac Newton"[4], he
describes Newton's achievement with notable precision:—

> All intellectual eye, our solar round
> First gazing through, he, by the blended power
> Of gravitation and projection, saw
> The whole in silent harmony revolve.
> From unassisted vision hid, the moons
> To cheer remoter planets numerous formed,
> By him in all their mingled tracts were seen.
> He also fixed our wandering Queen of Night,
> Whether she wanes into a scanty orb,
> Or, waxing broad, with her pale shadowy light
> In a soft deluge overflows the sky.
> Her every motion clear-discerning, he

Adjusted to the mutual main and taught
Why now the mighty mass of waters swells
Resistless, heaving on the broken rocks,
And the full river turning – till again
The tide revertive, unattracted, leaves
A yellow waste of idle sands behind.

(39–56)

Thomson does not confine himself to the law of gravitation: as Dr Meadows has noted[5], he is careful to add the idea of projection with a precise initial velocity. "Newton's main achievement in the *Principia* was his explanation of planetary motions – the fundamental problem of astronomy since antiquity – on the basis of a few simple laws of mechanics'plus the postulate of a universal gravitational attraction. He showed, in fact, that so long as the planets were projected with the correct initial velocities their present orbits would follow as a necessary consequence." The main poetic achievement of Thomson was to combine this scientific precision with an equally precise rendering of his own visual and emotional sensibility in phrases like "her pale shadowy light/ In a soft deluge overflows the sky", or "a yellow waste of idle sands".

Thomson was only the first Scottish Newtonian poet. The influence persists, for instance, in the earliest extant work of a third major Scottish writer, Robert Fergusson (1750–1774). In 1765, David Gregory, nephew of the David Gregory already mentioned, died at St Andrews, where he had held the Chair of Mathematics from 1739 to 1764. Fergusson entered St Andrews in 1764, and there the one academic subject for which he is said to have shown special ability was mathematics. As a natural enough consequence, in 1765 he wrote "Elegy on the Death of Mr David Gregory, late Professor of Mathematics in the University of St Andrews"[6]. This is burlesque in the Habbie Simpson tradition, but it is significant that, even in burlesque, the young Fergusson was able to develop his theme genuinely in terms of the new mathematics:—

He could, by *Euclid*, prove lang sine
A ganging *point* compos'd a line;
By numbers too he cou'd divine
        Whan he did read,
That *three* times *three* just made up nine;
        But now he's dead.

(13–18)

Admittedly, the last four lines are no more than burlesque, but the first couplet has a more complex point. M. P. McDiarmid in a note on the passage comments[7]: "According to the method of fluxions, invented by Newton, magnitudes are supposed to be generated by motion – e.g., a line by the motion of a point – – – As the obscurity of the kind of demonstration employed by Newton was the main objection brought against the system by its critics – for example, by Bishop Berkeley – the Scots mathematicians, particularly Colin McLaurin, sought to 'establish the Method of Fluxions on Principles equally evident and unexceptionable with those of the antient Geometricians deduced after their Manner, in the most rigid form.' " It is this last point which explains Fergusson's reference to Euclid rather than Newton himself; he sees Newton's work as it had been developed and clarified by McLaurin.

None of these poets however is merely Newtonian, or rather their Newtonianism implied other qualities and interests, most notably those connected with commercial and agricultural improvement. For Ramsay this has already been demonstrated. For Fergusson, as will appear in a subsequent chapter, certain reservations must be made, but a second University poem "An Eclogue, to the Memory of Dr William Wilkie, late Professor of Natural Philosophy in the University of St Andrews"[8] (1772), commemorates a man trained in Newtonian science, who was also in his way a not uninteresting poet, author of *The Epigoniad* (1757), and more definitely a successful improving farmer:—

'Twas na for weel tim'd verse or sangs alane,
He bore the bell frae ilka shepherd swain.
Nature to him had gi'en a kindly lore,
Deep a' her mystic *ferlies* to explore:
For a' her secret workings he could gie
Reasons that wi' her principles agree.
Ye saw yoursell how weel his *mailin* thrave,
Ay better faugh'd an' snodit than the lave;
Lang had the *thristles* an' the *dockans* been
In use to wag their taps upo' the green,
Whare now his bonny riggs delight the view,
An' thrivin hedges drink the caller dew.   (59–70)

The reference to hedges in particular established that Wilkie's farm was enclosed and improved.

ii

At least partly because Thomson was a Scot, whose maturity post-dated the 1707 Union, he became the first important poet to write with a

British rather than a Scottish or English outlook. Almost certainly he was the author of "Rule, Britannia". The recurrent theme of his verse is the commercial, philosophic, scientific and literary achievement and potential of Britain in the seventeenth and early eighteenth century. This achievement he idealizes as being in full accord with the harmonious Nature of his poems, something which might even ultimately help to reshape man in the natural perfection from which long ago he had fallen. It was for this reason that he addressed England in terms like the following[9]:—

> Full are thy cities with the sons of art;
> And trade and joy, in every busy street,
> Mingling are heard: even Drudgery himself,
> As at the car he sweats, or dusty, hews
> The palace stone, looks gay. Thy crowded ports,
> Where rising masts an endless prospect yield,
> With labour burn, and echo to the shouts
> Of hurried sailor, as he hearty waves
> His last adieu, and, loosening every sheet,
> Resigns the spreading vessel to the wind.
> ("Summer", 1457–1466)

Thomson here certainly expresses part of the truth, but "trade" and "joy" are combined in a way which might not seem entirely convincing to later, more disillusioned, generations, or even to some of his own contemporaries. Tobias Smollett (1721–1771), for instance, another Scot resident in London, befriended by Thomson, to whom he was junior by some twenty years, consistently presents a different view. After he had completed his studies at Glasgow University, most of Smollett's adult life was spent in England or abroad, and he is usually regarded as an English novelist who happened to be born in the Lennox. The truth is somewhat different. Smollett certainly concerns himself chiefly with satiric portrayals of English society at home and overseas; the point of view however is generally that of an outsider; in Roderick Random, that of a Scottish surgeon, whose career in some ways parallels Smollett's own: in Humphry Clinker that of a Welsh squire, who is unimpressed by London and Bath, but who feels a particular affinity with Smollett's own part of Scotland, the Lennox and Strathclyde[10]:—

> "You must know I have a sort of national attachment to this
> part of Scotland — The great church dedicated to St Mongah,
> the river Clyde, and other particulars that smack of our Welch
> language and customs, contribute to flatter me with the notion,

that these people are the descendants of the Britons, who once possessed this country. Without all question, this was a Cumbrian kingdom: its capital was Dumbarton (a corruption of Dumbritton) which still exists as a royal borough, at the influx of the Clyde and Leven, ten miles below Glasgow.''

Smollett here shows the influence of Innes's *A Critical Essay on the Ancient Inhabitants of the Northern Parts of Britain or Scotland*, and the converse of Squire Bramble's position is that, in Smollett, Welsh often becomes a convenient disguise for the less popular (in South Britain, that is to say) Scottish point of view. Even in *Peregrine Pickle*, the allegedly English hero works in close collaboration with the elderly Welsh misanthrope, Cadwallader Crabtree, to explode the pretences of English society.

In *Humphry Clinker*, Matthew Bramble describes the same London as Thomson, but lays his emphasis on the less pleasant sides of capitalism and *laissez-faire* enterprise[11]:—

"A companionable man will, undoubtedly, put up with many inconveniencies for the sake of enjoying agreeable society. A facetious friend of mine used to say, the wine could not be bad, where the company was agreeable; a maxim which, however, ought to be taken *cum grano salis*; but what is the society of London, that I should be tempted, for its sake, to mortify my senses, and compound with such uncleanness as my soul abhors? All the people I see, are too much engrossed by schemes of interest or ambition, to have any room left for sentiment or friendship. Even in some of my old acquaintance, these schemes and pursuits have obliterated all traces of our former connexion — Conversation is reduced to party disputes, and illiberal altercation — Social commerce, to formal visits and card-playing — — — — Every person you deal with endeavours to over-reach you in the way of business; you are preyed upon by idle mendicants, who beg in the phrase of borrowing, and live upon the spoils of the stranger — Your tradesmen are without conscience, your friends without affection, and your dependants without fidelity."

Correspondingly, Smollett's first-hand account of the British seaman bears little resemblance to the more romantic picture drawn in *The Seasons*. Thomson emphasises liberty as the basis of British prosperity; it is Smollett in *Roderick Random* who shows that the basis of the prosperity was the slave trade from Africa to Latin America. The traffic in slaves formed the base, and gave impetus to, the triangle of trade on which

British commercial prosperity so greatly depended. In *Roderick Random*, Lieutenant Bowling does not reveal the object of his voyage until Random has committed himself and left England, but, when he discovers the object of the voyage, Random shows no hesitation or remorse, and his account of the actual voyage contains no more than a hint of irony[12]:—

> "We made the land of Guinea, near the mouth of the River Gambia, and trading along the coast as far to the southward of the line as Angola and Bengula, in less than six months disposed of the greatest part of our cargo, and purchased four hundred negroes, my adventure having been laid out in gold dust.
>
> Our complement being made up, we took our departure from Cape Negro, and arrived in the Rio de la Plata in six weeks, having met with nothing remarkable in our voyage, except an epidemic fever, not unlike the jail distemper, which broke out among our slaves and carried off a good many of the ship's company; among whom I lost one of my mates, and poor Strap had well-nigh given up the ghost. Having produced our passport to the Spanish governor, we were received with great courtesy, sold our slaves in a very few days, and could have put off five times the number at our own price; though we were obliged to smuggle the rest of our merchandise, consisting of European bale goods, which, however, we made shift to dispose of at a great advantage."

Smollett certainly intended us to notice that it was legal to sell living Africans, but not European manufactured goods. The reflection does not, however, seem to qualify his approval of the method by which Random at last won possession of the divine and virtuous Narcissa.

In fairness to Thomson, it must be added that he was aware of, and condemned, the traffic in slaves[13]:—

> that cruel trade
> Which spoils unhappy Guinea of her sons.
> ("Summer", 1019–1020)

Equally, he failed to emphasise the extent to which the trade formed a foundation for the liberty and prosperity which he extolled. His vision remained literary, philosophic and rural, based much more on his reading and his experiences as a boy in the Borders and as a man in literary London and on English country estates, than on the commercial facts of the world around him. He resembles Voltaire in that it is for her philosophers and poets that he most genuinely venerates England. The philosophers demonstrated the range and power of the disciplined speculative intellect; the poets, Shakespeare in particular, showing the corresponding powers of natural intuition[14]:—

> Fair thy renown
> In awful sages and in noble bards;
> Soon as the light of dawning Science spread
> Her orient ray, and waked the Muses' song,
> Thine is a Bacon, hapless in his choice,
> Unfit to stand the civil storm of state,
> And, through the smooth barbarity of courts,
> With firm but pliant virtue forward still
> To urge his course: him for the studious shade
> Kind Nature formed, deep, comprehensive, clear,
> Exact, and elegant; in one rich soul,
> Plato, the Stagyrite, and Tully joined.
> The great deliverer he, who from the gloom
> Of cloistered monks and jargon-teaching schools,
> Led forth the true philosophy, there long
> Held in the magic chain of words and forms
> And definitions void: he led her forth,
> Daughter of Heaven! that, slow-ascending still,
> Investigating sure the chain of things,
> With radiant finger points to Heaven again.
> The generous Ashley thine, the friend of man,
> Who scanned his nature with a brother's eye,
> His weakness prompt to shade, to raise his aim,
> To touch the finer movements of the mind,
> And with the moral beauty charm the heart.
> Why need I name thy Boyle, whose pious search
> Amid the dark recesses of his works,
> The great Creator sought? And why thy Locke,
> Who made the whole internal world his own?
> Let Newton, pure intelligence, whom God
> To mortals lent to trace his boundless works
> From laws sublimely simple, speak thy fame
> In all philosophy. For lofty sense,
> Creative fancy, and inspection keen
> Through the deep winding of the human heart
> Is not wild Shakespeare thine and nature's boast?
> Is not each great, each amiable muse
> Of classic ages in thy Milton met?   ("Summer", 1531–1568)

All the philosophers referred to – Bacon, Shaftesbury, Boyle, Locke, Newton – were English forerunners of the Enlightenment. Later in the century Robert Fergusson still chose as symbols of the highest intellect, the English poet and the English philosopher, who in Thomson's catalogue had occupied the supreme positions[15]:—

> For thof ye had as wise a snout on
> As *Shakespeare* or *Sir Isaac Newton*
> Your judgment fouk wou'd hae a doubt on,
>   I'll tak my aith,
> Till they cou'd see ye wi' a suit on
>   O gude Braid Claith.
>   ("Braid Claith", 49–54)

Times, however, had obviously changed: material prosperity had come to mean more than intellectual achievement: Fergusson, like Smollett, bears witness to the relative positions in the later Enlightenment of intellectual and financial achievement.

When Thomson in "Autumn" turns to the praise of Scotland, he begins from what, by contrast with England, is desolation[16]:—

> Where the Northern Ocean in vast whirls
> Boils round the naked melancholy isles
> Of farthest Thule, and the Atlantic surge
> Pours in among the stormy Hebrides.
>   (862–865)

Scotland, of course, has never consisted merely of the Shetlands and the Hebrides (neither of which Thomson had visited), and he rather conspicuously omits to mention the poets, historians and mathematicians who had preceded him. In the context of *The Seasons*, England represents fulfilment; Scotland, with her "incult forests", "by Nature's hand/ Planted of old", with her[17]

>   manly race
> Of unsubmitting spirit, wise, and brave,
> Who still through bleeding ages struggled hard
> (As well unhappy Wallace can attest,
> Great patriot-hero! ill requited chief!)
> To hold a generous undiminished state,
> Too much in vain!
>   (897–903)

and with her perpetual problem of emigration, represents potential only

– but potential which, with proper cultivation, was quite capable of attaining the level of England or Holland[18]:—

> Oh! is there not some patriot in whose power
> That best, that godlike luxury is placed,
> Of blessing thousands, thousands yet unborn,
> Through late posterity? some, large of soul,
> To cheer dejected Industry, to give
> A double harvest to the pining swain,
> And teach the labouring hands the sweets of toil?
> How, by the finest art, the native robe
> To weave; how, white as Hyperborean snow,
> To form the lucid lawn; with venturous oar
> How to dash wide the billow; nor look on,
> Shamefully passive, while Batavian fleets
> Defraud us of the glittering finny swarms
> That heave our friths and crowd upon our shores;
> How all-enlivening trade to rouse, and wing
> The prosperous sail from every growing port,
> Uninjured, round the sea-encircled globe;
> And thus, in soul united as in name,
> Bid Britain reign the mistress of the deep.
>
> (910–928)

Agricultural improvement, the establishment of tweed and linen manufactories, the exploitation of fishery resources, and a share of world trade – these are the not unreasonable aspirations which Thomson urged on his fellow-countrymen, who in turn were so soon to fulfil them. As agents for the process, he puts forward the names of Duncan Forbes of Culloden (1685–1747), and John, second Duke of Argyll and Greenwich (1678–1743). It is interesting, at least in terms of the present study, to note that this last is the Duke of Argyll whose intervention Scott in *The Heart of Midlothian* represents as helping to save the life of Effie Deans, and who afterwards established David Deans on an improved "fancy farm" in the Lennox. Scott and Thomson are at one in assessing the Duke's achievement.

Thomson writes by preference about the activities of the countryside, which were more immediately meaningful in terms of Scottish prospects and his own upbringing. The theme of *The Castle of Indolence*, the overthrow of Indolence by Industry, has an obvious relevance for Scotland in the early eighteenth century. When Sir Industry in Canto II sets out to overthrow the enchanter, it is from an improved, and obviously English, rural retreat that he emerges[19]:—

Nor from his deep retirement banished was
The amusing cares of rural industry.
Still, as with grateful change the seasons pass,
New scenes arise, new landskips strike the eye,
And all the enlivened country beautify:
Gay plains extend where marshes slept before;
O'er recent meads the exulting streamlets fly;
Dark frowning heaths grow bright with Ceres' store;
And woods imbrown the steep, or wave along the shore.

(II,xxvii)

It would be an oversimplification to suggest that the domain of Sir
Industry is England, that of Indolence, Scotland. The prisoners of
Indolence, however, for the most part are Scots and the enchanted landscape of Canto I is a development of the landscape of the Borders as
Thomson rather awkwardly had presented it in "Of a Country Life", his
first published set of verses, which appeared in 1720, long before his
departure for England[20]:—

Where no rude noise insults the listening ear;
Nought but soft zephyrs whispering through the trees,
Or the still humming of the painful bees;
The gentle murmurs of a purling rill,
Or the unwearied chirping of the drill;
The charming harmony of warbling birds,
Or hollow lowings of the grazing herds;
The murmuring stockdoves' melancholy coo,
When they their lovéd mates lament or woo;
The pleasing bleatings of the tender lambs,
Or the indistinct mumbling of their dams;
The musical discord of chiding hounds,
Whereto the echoing hill or rock resounds;
The rural mournful songs of lovesick swains,
Whereby they soothe their raging amorous pains;
The whistling music of the lagging plough,
Which does the strength of drooping beasts renew.

(4–20)

It would probably be fair to say that the contrast between the England of
his later experience and the Scotland of his memories was an important
factor, conscious or unconscious, in the composition of *The Castle of
Indolence*, as in that of *The Seasons*, and helped to give didactic as well as
imaginative force to the poem.[21]

NOTES

1. Burns Martin and J. W. Oliver (eds.), *The Works of Allan Ramsay* I (S.T.S., Edinburgh and London, 1945), 158–166.
2. Martin and Oliver, *op. cit.*, II (S.T.S., Edinburgh and London, 1953), 176–178.
3. *Newton Demands the Muse* (Princeton, 1946).
4. J. Logie Robertson (ed.), *James Thomson Poetical Works* (London, 1908), 436–442.
5. Meadows, *op. cit.*, 119.
6. M. P. McDiarmid (ed.), *The Poems of Robert Fergusson* II (S.T.S., Edinburgh and London, 1956), 1–2.
7. *op. cit.*, 248.
8. McDiarmid, *op. cit.*, 82–85.
9. Logie Robertson, *op. cit.*, 106.
10. Lewis M. Knapp (ed.), *The Expedition of Humphry Clinker* (London, 1966), 247.
11. Knapp, *op. cit.*, 122–123.
12. G. Saintsbury (ed.), *The Works of Tobias Smollett* III (*Roderick Random* III), 180–189 (Chapter 65).
13. Logie Robertson, *op. cit.*, 89.
14. Logie Robertson, *op. cit.*, 109–111.
15. McDiarmid, *op. cit.*, 82.
16. Logie Robertson, *op. cit.*, 163.
17. Logie Robertson, *op. cit.*, 164.
18. Logie Robertson, *op. cit.*, 165.
19. Logie Robertson, *op. cit.*, 288.
20. Logie Robertson, *op. cit.*, 494.
21. See also Mary Jane Scott, *James Thomson, Anglo-Scot: A reconsideration of his works in relation to the Scottish background* (unpublished Ph.D. thesis, University of Edinburgh, 1979).

CHAPTER IV

NATURAL MAN:
The Gaelic Poets and Ossian

Thomson's attitude to Scotland contradicts itself in a way which is paralleled in several later writers, most notably Walter Scott. On the one hand, he looked with approval for the rapid approximation of Scotland to England and Europe. Despite this, his verse kindled to its best when he celebrated the wildness, the natural, even heroic simplicities of Scottish life, and in particular the life of the Highlands and Islands. To all appearance, it would have been easy for him to reverse the terms in which he wrote; to make Scotland, in other words, the home of the uncorrupted, the natural, the romantic; England that of the artificial, the heartless, the hypocritical. His emotions and his imagination led him in one direction, his practical sense and personal interests in another.

The idea of Scotland, and especially the Highlands, as the home of simplicity and romance was well established in England by the middle of the eighteenth century, as may be seen in Collins's "An Ode on the Popular Superstitions of the Highlands of Scotland", written in 1749, and addressed to John Home, the future author of *Douglas*, on his approaching return from London to Edinburgh[1]:—

There, must thou wake perforce thy Doric quill;
   'Tis Fancy's land to which thou sett'st thy feet;
   Where still, 'tis said, the fairy people meet,
Beneath each birken shade, on mead or hill.
There, each trim lass, that skims the milky store,
   To the swart tribes their creamy bowls allots;
By night they sip it round the cottage door,
   While airy minstrels warble jocund notes.
There, every herd, by sad experience, knows ·
   How, wing'd with fate, their elf-shot arrows fly,
When the sick ewe her summer food foregoes,
   Or, stretch'd on earth, the heart-smit heifers lie.

Such airy beings awe the untutor'd swain:
   Nor thou, though learn'd, his homelier thoughts neglect;
Let thy sweet muse the rural faith sustain;
   These are the themes of simple, sure effect,
That add new conquests to her boundless reign,
And fill, with double force, her heart-commanding strain - - -

Nor need'st thou blush that such false themes engage
   Thy gentle mind, of fairer stores possest;
   For not alone they touch the village breast,
But fill'd, in elder time, the historic page.
   There, Shakespeare's self, with every garland crown'd,
Flew to those fairy climes his fancy sheen,
   In musing hour; his wayward sisters found,
And with their terrors drest the magic scene.
   From them he sung, when, 'mid his bold design,
Before the Scot, afflicted, and aghast!
   The shadowy kings of Banquo's fated line
Through the dark cave in gleamy pageant pass'd.
   Proceed! nor quit the tales which, simply told,
Could once so well my answering bosom pierce;
   Proceed, in forceful sounds, and colours bold,
The native legends of thy land rehearse;
To such adapt thy lyre, and suit thy powerful verse.

In scenes like these, which, daring to depart
   From sober truth, are still to nature true,
   And call forth fresh delight to Fancy's view,
The heroic muse employ'd her Tasso's art!

(18–35; 172–192)

Collins makes an explicit distinction between external scientific and philosophic truth, which satisfies the intellect, and which, at least by implication, belongs to the England of Locke and Newton, and internal natural truth, which in a scientific or philosophical sense may not be truth at all, but which convinces the imagination, and to which the achievement of Shakespeare and Tasso has given an authority equal to that of the scientific. For him, the home of this latter kind of truth is Scotland. His position is related to that of Thomson, but the value which he sets on the two kinds of truth is quite different.

In Scotland itself, despite a number of earlier attempts, the full development of Collins's idea was reserved for the end of the century and the beginning of the next; one might almost say, for "Tam O'

Shanter" and "Wandering Willie's Tale". The earlier tendency was to
see Scotland as the realm of Nature and natural man. Home, for
example, in *Douglas* concentrated on natural man[2]:—

> *Lord Randolph.* Whoe'er thou art, thy spirit is ennobl'd
> By the great King of Kings! thou art ordain'd
> And stamp'd a hero by the sovereign hand
> Of Nature! blush not, flower of modesty
> As well as valour, to declare thy birth.

> *Stranger.* My name is Norval: on the Grampian hills
> My father feeds his flocks; a frugal swain,
> Whose constant cares were to increase his store,
> And keep his only son, myself, at home.
>
> (II, 39–47)

The kinship, or at least the former kinship, of the natural with
Scotland and the Scottish language forms the underlying theme of
Ramsay's Preface to *The Ever Green* (1724), where by implication much
even of the best English Augustan poetry receives abrupt dismissal[3]:—

"I have observed that *Readers* of the best and most exquisite
Discernment frequently complain of our *modern Writings*, as
filled with affected Delicacies and studied Refinements, which
they would gladly exchange for that natural Strength of
Thought and Simplicity of Stile our Forefathers practised: to
such, I hope, the following *Collection of Poems* will not be
displeasing.

When these good old *Bards* wrote, we had not yet made Use
of imported Trimmings upon our Cloaths, nor of Foreign
Embroidery in our Writings. Their *Poetry* is the Product of
their own Country, not pilfered and spoiled in the
Transportation from abroad: Their *Images* are native, and their
Landskips domestick; copied from those Fields and Meadows we
every Day behold.

The *Morning* rises (in the Poets Description) as she does in the
Scottish Horizon. We are not carried to *Greece* or *Italy* for a
Shade, a Stream or a Breeze. The *Groves* rise in our own
Valleys; the *Rivers* flow from our own Fountains, and the *Winds*
blow upon our own Hills. I find not Fault with those Things, as
they are in *Greece* or *Italy*: But with a *Northern Poet* for fetching
his Materials from these Places, in a Poem, of which his own
Country is the Scene; as our *Hymners* to the *Spring* and *Makers of
Pastorals* frequently do."　　　　　　　　　　　(IV, 236)

Ramsay was himself a Maker of Pastorals, but to his contemporaries one of the startling effects of *The Gentle Shepherd* was its realism, its concern with men and women who were shepherds of necessity and upbringing, and spoke in an approximation to the language of real shepherds; who were portrayed as living at a definite time and place and in definite historical circumstances. Similarly, when he came to render Horace, Ramsay translated landscape, personal references and virtually everything else into terms of his own Scotland, with results and implications discussed in a later section of this book.

Smollett's attitude to southern England in general and London in particular, has already been discussed; his attitude to Scotland is very different. In *Humphry Clinker* it receives expression chiefly by way of Matthew Bramble. The main attraction is the pastoral landscape, but that is not all. The Scottish legal and medical professions outshine those of England; "Edinburgh is a hot-bed of genius"; Mr Bramble is "in raptures with Glasgow"; in Glasgow University "their mode of education is certainly preferable to ours in some respects"[4]. But it is the pastoral, and more especially the wilder parts of Scotland around Loch Lomond, that have the greatest appeal and offer the maximum beneficial contrast to London and Bath. Matthew Bramble's inclination, characteristically, is for the pastoral, and embodies a good deal of practical information[5]:—

> "Every thing here is romantic beyond imagination. This country is justly styled the Arcadia of Scotland; and I don't doubt but it may vie with Arcadia in everything but climate – I am sure it excels it in verdure, wood and water – What say you to a natural bason of pure water, near thirty miles long, and in some places seven miles broad, and in many above a hundred fathom deep, having four and twenty habitable islands, some of them stocked with deer, and all of them covered with wood; containing immense quantities of delicious fish, salmon, pike, trout, perch, flounders, eels, and powans, the last a delicate kind of fresh-water herring peculiar to this lake; and finally communicating with the sea, by sending off the Leven, through which all those species (except the powan) make their exit and entrance occasionally?"

In the same letter Bramble "quotes" Smollett's own classical "Ode to Leven-Water"[6]:—

> Still on thy banks so gaily green
> May num'rous herds and flocks be seen,
> And lasses chanting o'er the pail,

> And shepherds piping in the dale,
> And ancient faith that knows no guile,
> And industry imbrown'd with toil,
> And hearts resolv'd, and hands prepar'd
> The blessings they enjoy to guard.

In a measure, Smollett's classical style and references contradict Ramsay's dictum already quoted. Such references and reminiscences, however, strengthen rather than weaken the effect of the natural. Classical Greece was the country where poets and artists had most clearly set down the true face of Nature; and in Greece it was not so much in Athens during the period of Attic dominance as in the earlier, less sophisticated Homeric period, or in the less sophisticated areas of Dorian (Doric) speech, that Nature had found her most complete expression. Theocritus, Pindar, Homer – masters respectively of the pastoral, the ode, and the epic – were the great exemplars of the natural in poetry. For Scots, the parallel of Greece with Britain was clear. The literature of eighteenth century London and England corresponded to that of classical Athens; in Scotland was to be found not only the landscape, but also the society, the languages, and the literatures which possessed qualities analogous to those of Greece outside Attica. In Scotland, two non-Attic languages survived and flourished – Lowland Scots, which even today is familiarly referred to as the Doric, and Gaelic. These languages it was felt, were specially capable of expressing the thoughts and emotions of natural man. Eighteenth century interest in Scots and Gaelic was thus closely connected with enquiries into human nature, and the development of the moral sciences, which formed the central concerns of Hume's *Treatise*, Ferguson's *Essay* and Rousseau's *Émile* and *Du Contrat social*.

Burns on occasion consciously played the part of Lowland Scots Natural Man. During the century, however, there was an increasing tendency to equate National Man, not so much with the inspired rustic as with the Noble Savage. The tendency was by no means universal, as Voltaire's *Entretiens d'un sauvage et d'un bachelier* (1761) or Adam Ferguson's treatment of the State of Nature will illustrate[7]:—

> "If we admit that man is susceptible of improvement, and has
> in himself a principle of progression, and a desire of perfection,
> it appears improper to say, that he has quitted the state of his
> nature, when he has begun to proceed; or that he finds a station
> for which he was not intended, while, like other animals, he
> only follows the disposition, and employs the powers that
> nature has given."

Even Ferguson, however, drew many, perhaps most, of his examples from relatively primitive societies. The majority of educated people were susceptible to the appeal of the Noble Savage.

ii

It is wrong to draw too firm a distinction between Lowland and Highland Scotland, or to equate the latter too readily with the primitive ideal. Scott, as usual, is precise when in *Rob Roy*[8] he links the Glasgow magistrate, Baillie Nicol Jarvie, and the Highland cateran, Rob Roy himself, by "the auld wife ayont the fire at Stuckavrallachan, that made some mixture of our bluids". The pair are full cousins. The relationship symbolizes that of the two linguistic groups in Scotland, and at the same time is modelled on the historical connection between Rob Roy and his cousins in Aberdeen and Edinburgh, the mathematical and medical Gregories whose name has so often appeared in this study. (The surname had been slightly altered to avoid the seventeenth-century proscription of the name MacGregor.) Nor were the Gregories the only Gaels to achieve something like full European intellectual eminence. George Buchanan had been a native Gaelic-speaker, and one of his main achievements as a historian, the establishment of the linguistic connection between Scotland, Wales and Ireland on the one hand, and on the other such areas of Gaulish settlement in Europe and Asia as France, Spain, northern Italy, the Danube valley and Galatia in Asia Minor – the concept, that is to say, of a Celtic group of languages and peoples, still important in comparative linguistics and archaeology – depends as much on his native knowledge of Gaelic as on his classical scholarship[9]. Buchanan was the first to use the word "Celtic" in the modern sense. Robert Kirk, Colin McLaurin and Adam Fergusson were all native Gaelic-speakers, and although neither McLaurin nor Fergusson, so far as is known, made any attempt at scientific or literary work in the language, some of Kirk's published work is in Gaelic.

Gaelic bardic poetry in the seventeenth century was intensely traditional, and as a consequence in the work of the best known poets almost confined to the linked genres of panegyric, satire and elegy. At the same time it was very much a poetry of the present, of individual events as they impinged on a society whose institutions had been stable for a long time. The dominant image, as in *"An Talla am bu ghnath le MacLeoid"*[10] ("MacLeod's Wonted Hall") by Mary MacLeod (*c.* 1615–*c.* 1705), is the wealth, culture and hospitality of the medieval great house, which still survived in many parts of Scotland:—

An ám dhuit tighinn gu d'bhaile
Is tu bu tighernail gabhail,
An uair a shuidheadh gach caraid mu d'bhòrd.

Bha thu measail aig uaislean,
Is cha robh beagan mar chruas ort:
Sud an cleachdamh a fhuair thu ad aois òig.

Gum biodh farum air thàilisg
Agus fuaim air a' chlàrsaich
Mar a bhuineadh do shàr mhac Mhic Leoid.

Gur h-e bu eachdraidh 'na dhéidh sin
Greis air ursgeil na Féinne,
Is air chuideachda chéirghil nan cròc.

(273–284)

"When you came to your chieftain's house, it is you who were gracious in behaviour, when every friend was seated round your table.

Among nobles you were esteemed, and no little thing upset you; such was your custom from the time of your youth.

The chessmen would rattle and the harp would be sounding, as was meet for MacLeod's noble son.

After that for a while would be told the story of the Fiann, and of the white-buttocked antlered band."

Elegy equally is dominated by the desolation of the great house, as in the lament for Alexander MacDonald, Chief of Keppoch, who was murdered in 1663. The poet is Iain Lom[11] (John MacDonald: *c.* 1624–*c.* 1710):—

Tha do shèomartaigh duinte
Gun aon smùid ann no cèo.
(1006–1007: "*Murt na Ceapaich*")

"Your chambered house is closed – there is no smoke or reek from it."
The image is taken up and transcended by Mary MacLeod in a magnificent stanza from the "*Marbhrann*"[12], "Dirge", for Iain Garbh of Raasay, who was drowned in 1671 during a voyage from Lewis to his home:—

Is e dh'fhàg silteach mo shùil
Faicinn t'fhearainn gun sùrd
Is do bhaile gun smùid
Fo charraig nan sùgh,
Dheagh mhic Chaluim nan tùr á Ratharsaidh.

(327–331)

"What has left my eyes full of tears is to see your land cheerless and your chieftain's house without smoke under the rock where the waves beat, excellent son of Calum of the towers from Raasay."

The middle and later seventeenth century witnessed the beginning of the upheavals which eventually destroyed this traditional society, at least on the higher social level, yet to compare the poetry of Mary MacLeod or Iain Lom with that of their approximate Lowland contemporaries, Drummond and Pitcairn, is to be struck by the confidence of the Gaels in the permanence, as well as the excellence, of the old order, even when it was visibly crumbling before their eyes. Here and there, as for instance in the "*Oran do Mhac Leoid Dhun Bheagain*"[13], "Song to MacLeod of Dunvegan", by Roderick Morison, the Blind Harper (*c.* 1656–*c.* 1714), there is some consciousness of change, but more typical is Iain Lom's lament for Claverhouse, which has none of the eschatological overtones of Pitcairne[14]:—

> *Ceannard an àigh, gun do thuit thu 'sa' bhlàr!*
>   *'S bu sgathach do làmh gus an tàinig an uair;*
> *'S e do bhàs, a Dhùn-dighe, dh'fhàg ormsa trom-lighe,*
>   *Chuir toll ann mo chridhe 's a dh'fhàg snigh' air mo ghruaidh;*
> *Bu bheag air son t'èirig na thuit de na bèisdean,*
>   *An cogadh Rìgh Seumas ged dh'èirich leinn buaidh;*
> *Ach sgapadh nan cuileag air muinntir Rìgh Uilleam,*
>   *Tha sinne fo mhulad ged chuir sinn iad uainn.*
>   (2402–2409: "*Oran air Feachd Rìgh Seumas*")

"Beloved leader, alas that you fell in battle! Trenchant was your sword-hand till the hour of death came. It is your death, Dundee, that has left grief upon me, that has pierced my heart and made the tears course on my cheek. Although we won the victory in the cause of King James, all the brutes that fell would be little as blood-price for your death. But King William's forces were brushed off like flies, and although we drove them away from us, we are under a load of sorrow."

Like Dryden before him, Iain Lom drew a parallel between events of his own day and the Old Testament story of the revolt against David by his son Absalom. For Dryden, Absalom was the Duke of Monmouth, David represented Charles II, and the tragic outcome was deliberately fudged. For Iain Lom, David represented James VII and Absalom was his son-in-law William II. Iain may well, I suppose, have read his Dryden, but with an irony which hindsight allows us to appreciate, he makes no attempt to avoid the end of the story[15]:—

Bha mac aig Rìgh Dàibhidh
'S bu deas àill air ceann sluaigh e,
Chaidh an aghaidh an athar,
'S am fear nach catharr' d'a bhuaireadh;
'N uair a sgaoileadh am blàr sin
Thug Dia pàigheadh 'na dhuais da,
'S on bu droch dhuine cloinn' e,
Chroch a' choill' air a ghruaig e.

Ach buaidh an droch sgeòil sin
Do Phrionns Orainns gun diadhachd!
(2640–2649: *"Oran air Rìgh Ulleam agus Banrìgh Mairi"*)

"King David had a son, and erect and handsome was he at the head of a host, who opposed a father, incited by the Alien One. When the battle came to an end, God gave him his deserts. Because he was an evil son, the tree hanged him by the hair. May the efficacy of that tale be true of this ungodly Prince of Orange."

Culloden and the reprisals which followed finally put an end to such confidence, and the poetic style in which it had found expression. It is remarkable how swift a rebirth followed, marked in 1751 by the publication in Edinburgh of a volume in which Gaelic poems for the first time were printed rather than performed and circulated orally or in manuscript, a volume significantly entitled *Aiseiridh na Sean Chànoin Albannaich*, "Resurrection of the Ancient Scottish Tongue" by Alasdair Mac Mhaighstir Alasdair (Alexander MacDonald, c. 1690–c. 1770). The book opens with a panegyric, not of a chief, but of Gaelic as the natural uncorrupt speech of men to whom God has given language as his greatest gift. Mac Mhaighstir Alasdair ignores English (or Scots), and compares Gaelic favourably with Latin, Greek and French; indeed, he claims, following the arguments of David Malcolm, minister of Duddingston from 1705–1743, that all other languages derive from it, that it antedates Babel, and was the language of the Garden of Eden[16]:—

'S a réir Mhic Comb
An t'ùghdar mòr ri luaidh,
'S i 's freumhach òir
'S ceud ghràmar glòir gach sluaigh.
(129–132)

"According to Malcolm, the great celebrated author, it is the golden root and the first grammar of speech for every people."

More significant, and more seriously intended perhaps, is the concept already implicit in the title of the book, that Gaelic is the natural language of Scotland as a whole. " 'S i labhair Gaill is Gàidheil" (53), "It was the language of Lowlander and Highlander", he claims, and refers in justification to the reign of Malcolm Canmore (1057–1093), the last ruler of a kingdom, corresponding more or less in area to the modern Scotland, which used Gaelic as its ordinary court language. Later history, leading as it did to the Glorious Revolution, the Union of Parliaments, the Hanoverian succession and Culloden is by implication a long process of decline, reversible only by the resurrection of Gaelic and the restoration of the House of Stewart. The book was printed and published in Edinburgh with a preface in English to symbolize, it may be, that its language and contents were of national importance. Most of the verse is strongly Jacobite; all copies still in the hands of the printer were burnt by the common hangman in Edinburgh in 1752. Despite this, no action was taken against the poet, perhaps because the total effect is more messianic than activist. Mac Mhaighstir Alasdair is not himself a sentimental Jacobite of the later pattern, but the first symptoms of that disease are visible in his political poetry[17]:—

> Thig soinnion leis an rìgh,
> Teichidh sneachd is eire bhuainn;
> Fògrar dòruinn shìon,
> Thig sòlas, falbhaidh pian;
> Gach seòrsa de gach fìon,
> Thig bho 'n Fhraing 'n a thunnaichean,
> 'S gu 'n caisg sinn uil' ar n-ìot:
> Gheibh sinn tuil de 'r miann,
> 'S mu 'r naimhdean dh'fhag sinn uireasbhach,
> 'S dlùth chuireas sinn ar lìon.
> ("Oran mu Bhliadhna Thearlaich", 11–20)

"Sunshine will come with the king, snow and frost will flee from us; vexation of weather will be banished, joy will come, distress will go; every kind of wine will come from France by the barrel, so that we shall all put an end to our thirst: we shall find a flood of our desire, and around our enemies who left us in want, we shall set our net tight."

The imagery combining, as it does, Isaiah and the Land of Cockaigne, virtually relegates the return of the king to the end of the world, or to the recovery of some lost paradise.

But it was not entirely Paradise Lost. Gaelic, it will be remembered, was for Mac Mhaighstir Alasdair the language of Eden, and for him

Eden survived in the Highland landscape, which Thomson had described as barren, but which he saw under a different light. In several of his poems he gives marvellous expression to the crowded vitality of this landscape. They demonstrate the survival of Paradise, more or less wherever traditional Gaelic life had also survived, in Morar ("*Failte na Mòrthir*"), in "a certain township in Ardnamurchan called the Mill Corrie" ("*Allt an t-Siùcair*"), or in Inverie on the Knoydart coast, to which he had been forced to flit from the horrors of Eigneig in Glenuig[18]:—

> *Baile gun ghlaistig, gun bhòcan,*
> *'S coisrigte gach crann is fòid deth,*
> *Gun deanntag, gun charran, gun fhòtus,*
> *Lom-lan chluaran, lilidh, 's ròsan.*
>
> *A mhaghan a' bòrcadh le neòinean,*
> *Stràcte le deagh mheasan òirdheirc*
> *Cha chinn lus bhios searbh am fòid deth;*
> *Barrach, bainneach, mealach, sòbhrach — — —*
>
> *Failte ort fhèin a Phàrrais fhaoilidh,*
> *Ionbhar-Aoidh, am baile tlachdmhor.*
> ("*Imrich Alastair a Eigneig*", 37–44, 61–62)

"A township with no she-devil or hobgoblin, and consecrated is each tree and turf of it; without nettle, without spurrey, without refuse; brimfull of corn-marigold, lily and rose.

Its fields blossoming with daisy, filled with good and worthy fruit; no bitter herb grows on its soil; it is heaped-up, milky, honied, abounding in primroses — — —

Hail to you, hospitable Paradise, Inverie the delightful township."

The land is unimproved but productive — "*baile blàth, 's math fàs gach seòrs' ann*" (49), "warm township, with good increase of every kind in it", is the phrase used. The bard sees in it a little domain of teeming life, productivity and beauty, as yet unthreatened by the Whigs and Hanoverians who had oppressed him at Eigneig.

More general are his poems on Summer and Winter, the first a celebration of Beltane, May-day, which in Celtic belief marked the mid-point of the year, the beginning of summer[19]:—

> *A Bhealltainn bhog-bhailceach, ghrianach,*
> *Lònach, lianach, mo ghràidh.*
> ("*Oran an t-Samhraidh*", 89–90)

"Beltane of soft rain and sunshine, of meadows and fields, my love."
The poem is encyclopaedic; almost a natural history in the tradition of
Morison and Sibbald, an attempt to express the Highland ecology in a
vocabulary as rich and varied as the subject-matter itself. The song to
Winter is more dynamic in structure. The disruption caused by winter is
expressed in a stream of metaphors based mainly on traditional
aristocratic society, with such institutions as fosterage and mail (a word
also found in Scots – "customary rent", originally paid in kind) almost
totally dependent on the maternal goodness of the clan territory[20]:—

> Cuirear daltachan srian-bhuidh' nan ròs
> Bhàrr mìn-chioch nan òr-dhithein beag,
> Sinean gucagach lilidh nan lòn,
> Nam flùran 's geal-neòinean nan eag,
> Cha deòghlar le beachain nam bruach,
> Cròidhidh fuarachd car cuairt iad 'nan sgeap;
> Cha mhò chruinnicheas seillein a mhàl,
> 'S thar geal ùr-ros chrann gàraidh cha streap.
>
> (40–47)

"The yellow-streaked fosterlings of the roses will be weaned from the
soft breast of the little gold flowers; the swelling teats of the meadow-
lilies, and of the flowers and white daisies of the nooks, will not be
sucked by the bee of the verges; dampness will keep them home for a
time in their skep; no more will the bee gather his mail, nor will he climb
over the white fresh rose of the trees in the garden."

An image which certainly belongs to the *ancien régime* is the extraordinary one of the sun as valet – a kind of Figaro to the Almaviva of the
heather:—

> A fhraoich, bhadanaich, ghaganaich dhlùth,
> Do 'm b' ola 's do 'm fhùdar a mhil,
> B' i bhlàth ghrian do valet 's gach uair,
> Gu giullachd do ghruaige le sgil.
>
> (73–76)

"Tufted, close-clustered heather, for whom honey is oil and powder,
the sun in his warmth served continually as your valet to prepare your
wig adeptly."

Nature is seen too in terms of a church older and more ceremonious
than the Presbyterian:—

> Togaich bùirdeisich sgiathach nan speur,
> De 'n ceileireadh grianach car greis;

Cha sheinn iad am maidnean gu h-àrd,
No 'm feasgarain chràbhach 'sa phreas.

(33–36)

"The winged burgesses of the skies will cease from their warbling for a while; they will not sing matins on high, nor vespers devout in the bush."

The image occurs in this form near the beginning of the poem; when at the end the return of summer is mentioned, it recurs with greater elaboration:—

'S theid gach salmadair ball-mhaiseach, ùr,
An crannaig chùbhraidh chraoibh dlùth-dhuilleach cas;
Le 'n seòl féin a sheinn hymns, 's a thoirt cliù,
Chionn a' planet so chùrsadh air ais;
Gu 'm bi còisir air leth anns gach géig,
An dasgan éibhinn air réidh-shlios nan slat,
A' toirt lag-ìobairt le 'n ceileir do 'n Triath.

(129–135)

"Every beautiful-limbed young psalm-singer will go to the fragrant pulpit in the close-leaved tall tree, to sing hymns in their manner, and to give praise because this planet" (i.e. the sun) "would move in its course back (to summer); there will be a separate choir on every branch, with their jolly desks on the smooth side of the twigs, making a feeble offertory to the Lord with their warbling."

As the images conjure up a society which, when the poem was written, was already dead or dying, so the astronomical movements which bring about the seasonal disruption are described in terms of the old rather than the new science, which by Mac Mhaighstir Alasdair's time was not so very new, and with which he, as an educated man who had been a student at Glasgow University, must have been familiar. Yet the opening of the poem brings to mind Buchanan's *De Sphaera* rather than the works of Galileo or Newton. The two seasonal poems are often supposed to have been influenced by James Thomson, and I think it entirely possible that this is so; apart from the subject matter, which is not readily paralleled in earlier Gaelic poetry, the English words which appear with unusual frequency, especially in the song to Winter – "planet", "globe", "sign", "tropic", "hymns", "Phoebus" – are all favourites with Thomson. The astronomy however is so different that it must, I suggest, reflect a conscious decision on the poet's part to make use of a science appropriate to the golden age which provided a subject-matter for his metaphors. The pre-eminence accorded Buchanan in

seventeenth and eighteenth century Scotland might suggest indeed that
he had read *De Sphaera* and decided for nationalistic or other reasons to
make use of its doctrines:—

> *Tharruing grian, rìgh nan* planet *'s nan reul*
> *Gu sign Chancer Diciadaoin, gu beachd,*
> *A riaghlas cothrom mu 'n chriochnaich e thriall,*
> *Dà mhìos deug na bliadhna mu seach;*
> *Ach gur h-e 'n dara Di-Sathurn 'na dhéigh,*
> *A' ghrianstad-shamhraidh, aon deug an la 's fàid';*
> *'S an sin tionndaigh e chùrsa gu seamh,*
> *Gu seasghrian a' gheamhraidh gun stad.*

(1–8)

"The sun, king of the planets and stars, who rules equitably the twelve
months of the year, each in rotation before he finishes his journey,
reached the sign of Cancer on Wednesday; but it is the second Saturday
following, the summer solstice, the eleventh" (of June, O.S.) "which is
the longest day; at that time, quietly, without pause, he will turn his
course towards the solstice of winter."

The metaphorical structure suggests that Mac Mhaighstir Alasdair
found in the two opposed seasons an image of Gaelic and Scottish
society; in summer the original paradisal state, which had been lost,
although not permanently, because the nature of the creation ensured an
eventual resurrection. The word *aiseirigh*, "resurrection", which appears
in the title of the volume, reappears in the final stanza of the song to
Winter:—

> *Cha bhi creutair fo chopan nan speur,*
> *'N sin nach tionndaigh gu spéirid, 's ri 'n dreach;*
> *'S gu 'n toir Phoebus le buadhan a bhlàis,*
> *Anam-fàis daibh is càileachdan ceart;*
> *'S ni iad aiseirigh choitchionn a 'n uaigh,*
> *Far 'n do mheataich am fuachd iad a steach;*
> *'S their iad guileag – doro-hidala-hann,*
> *Dh'fhalbh an geamhradh 's tha 'n samhradh air teachd!*

(137–144)

"There isn't a creature beneath the vault of the heavens but will return
to vigour and their own beauty; Phoebus by the virtues of his heat will
give them power of growth and proper state of being; they will make a
communal resurrection from their grave where the cold enclosed them
in feebleness, and they will give a cry of joy – 'Doro-hidala-hann,
winter has gone, summer is come!'"

The 144 lines of the poem may have a numerological significance. 144 is 12^2, and the most obvious connection is with the twelve months of the year, or perhaps rather the twelve signs of the Zodiac. Four are mentioned; Cancer, the sign of the summer solstice, in the second line of the first stanza; Capricorn, the sign of the winter solstice, in a precisely corresponding place twelve stanzas or six months later (line 90); Taurus, the second spring sign, in the last line but one of the eleventh stanza (line 87), and Gemini, the third spring sign, in the fifth line of the sixteenth stanza (line 125). But this may not be all. If, as I have suggested, the movement of the poem from summer through winter to summer is to be equated with Gaelic and even perhaps human history, from Paradise through Paradise Lost to the *aiseirigh choitchionn a 'n uaigh*, the "general resurrection from their grave" of the final stanza just quoted, and so to Paradise Regained, some connection with the eschatology of the New Testament *Revelation* is at least possible. The structure of *Revelation* is more firmly numerological than that of any other book of the New Testament, and much is based on numbers which are also conspicuous in the poem, 12, 24 (2×12) and 144 $(12^2)^{21}$:—

"Twelve, the product of four and three, is most conspicuous in connection with the bride of the Lamb, New Jerusalem (XXI–XXII). The city has twelve gates, three in each of the four walls, and each gate is named for one of the twelve tribes of Israel. It has twelve foundations, each named after one of the twelve apostles. In form, the city is a cube, with a length and breadth and height of twelve thousand furlongs (1500 miles!). The height of the wall, as opposed perhaps to the height of the city, is 144 cubits (144 = 12×12; cf. the 144,000 who in VII are sealed), but it is worthy noticing that the cubits are to be measured in terms of the arm of an angel (XXI, 17); 144 angelic cubits may be equivalent to twelve thousand earthly furlongs. The precious stones which make up the twelve foundations are those which were believed to have a mystic correspondence with the twelve signs of the Zodiac, but, for whatever reason, John places them in an order precisely the reverse of that usually found in astrological records. Within the city grows the Tree of Life, 'which bare twelve manner of fruits, and yielded her fruit every month: and the leaves of the tree were for the healing of the nations' (XXII, 2).

Twenty-four is most conspicuous in the description of the heavenly throne and its setting, which forms chapter IV. Twenty-four elders are seated about the throne, and each of the

four beasts, who are also present, has six wings. The figure
twenty-four may, I suggest, represent the sum of the hours of
the day, which, like that of the days of the week, on occasions
represents the completed course of time."

It may well be, in other words, that the formal qualities of the poem
indicate that it is something more than seasonal, and in fact is prophetic
and apocalyptic. The messianic note in "*Oran mu Bhliadhna Thearlaich*"
has already been mentioned, and it should also be added that the
movement from life to death to resurrection corresponds to that from
calm to storm to renewed calm and arrival in harbour in Mac Mhaighstir
Alasdair's most celebrated poem, *Birlinn Chlannraghnaill*[22], "The Galley
of Clanranald".

Numerology as a serious literary device belongs essentially to the
Middle Ages and the Renaissance, the best-known Scottish examples
being[23] the *Altus Prosator* of Columba (*c.* 521–597), the *Kingis Quair* of
James I (1394–1437), the *New Orpheus* of Robert Henryson, and the *Palice
of Honour* of Gavin Douglas (*c.* 1475–1522). (To these should now be
added Drummond's "An Hymne of the Fairest Faire".) If it exists in Mac
Mhaighstir Alasdair's poem, it is another example of the creative way in
which he linked his work to the past in anticipation of a restorative and
transcendent future.

iii

Mac Mhaighstir Alasdair was a man of education and considerable
general culture. In this, as in other ways, he stands in marked contrast to
the other great Gaelic poet of the century, Donnchadh Ban Mac an t-
Saoir (1724–1812), who could neither read nor write, and who spent
much of his adult life in the Lowlands as a soldier and member of the
Edinburgh City Guard. Yet he too is affected by contemporary Lowland
and European ideas. In *Oran do'n Righ*[24] (*Song to the King*), for instance,
written in the early part of the reign of George III (1760–1820), he
says:—

> 'S mór a rinn e dh'fhearas-taighe,
> Sgaoil e h-uile mathas òirnne:
> Chuir e drochaid air gach alltan,
> 'S réitich e na rathaidean móra;
> Chuir e sgoil 's a h-uile gleann
> A los gum faigheadh ar clann fòghlam.
> (445–450)

"Much has he done in home affairs, he has showered all benefits upon
us, he has placed a bridge on every burn, and he has made the highways

smooth; he has set a school in every glen, so that our children might have schooling."

The juxtaposition of practical and intellectual improvement is very characteristic of the Scottish Enlightenment. (In the last couplet there may be a wry recognition of his own illiteracy.) One of his panegyrics[25] is addressed to John Campbell, *Iain Caimbeul a' bhanca*, who in 1745 became principal cashier of the Royal Bank of Scotland in Edinburgh:—

> *Fhuair thu mios nach'eil bitheant'*
> *A miosg Bhreatannach,*
> *Banc an òir bhith fo d' sgòid*
> *Ann an còir dhleasdanaich.*

(661–664)

"You have received an honour rare among British folk – a gold-stocked bank put under your sway, by the title of office."

It is worth observing that, in a poem on a man who was a characteristic figure of the Enlightenment and the improvements which accompanied it, Donnchadh Bàn consciously or unconsciously follows Thomson's example, and sees his subject in terms, not of Highlands and Lowlands, nor even Scotland and England, but of Britain as a whole.

Traces of the Enlightenment, however, are much less conspicuous than the idealization of a past aristocratic and heroic society, whose dual activities had been hunting and hospitality. The fact that John Campbell was a banker is soon forgotten; he is praised as generous chief, horseman and warrior, in a way to discourage anyone with evil designs on the Royal Bank:—

> *B' e do roghainn a dh' armachd*
> *An targaid chruinn ùr*
> *Gu meanbhbhallach dlùth*
> *Buidhe tairgneach cruaidh seòlt';*
> *Is claidheamh chinn airgid*
> *Cruaidh calma, nach lùb,*
> *Lann thana gheur chùil*
> *Gu daingean ad dhòrn;*
> *Mar ri dag, ullamh ghrad,*
> *A bhiodh a snap freasdalach,*
> *Nach biodh stad air a sraid*
> *Ach bhith mach freagarrach;*
> *Fùdar cruaidh sgeilcearra*

> *Am feadan glé dhìreach*
> *Ad làmhan geal' mine,*
> *'S cuilìobhair, caol gorm.*
>
> (685–700)

"This was thy choice of arms – the new circular targe with close-set small bosses, yellow, studded, firm, cunningly wrought; sword of the silver hilt, hard, sturdy and rigid; a thin, keen back blade held fast in thy fist; with a primed, swift-acting pistol, whereof the cock would be ready and the spark not delayed, but flashing responsively; then powder, hard-grained, explosive, in a dead true barrel, gripped in thy smooth white hands; and a slender, blue musket withal."

The chief effect of the Enlightenment on Highland society was the conscious and apparently rational destruction of the old order by the prohibition of arms and the Highland dress, and, more positively, by the introduction of sheep-farming, with the consequent destruction of agricultural communities – the Clearances, as the process came to be called. Donnchadh Bàn is aware of, and bitterly resents all this. His *Oran nam Balgairean*[26] ("Song to the Foxes"), for instance, praises the foxes, who destroy the sheep, which "cause dispeace throughout the world":—

> *Na bailtean is na h-àirighean*
> *Am faighte blàths is faoileachd,*
>
> *Gun taighean ach na làraichean*
> *Gun àiteach air na raointean*
>
> *Tha h-uile seòl a b'àbhaist*
> *Anns a' Ghaidhealtachd air caochladh*
>
> *Air cinntinn cho mì-nàdurra*
> *'Sna h-àitean a bha aoigheil*
>
> (5031–5038)

"The villages and shielings where warmth and cheer were found, have no houses save the ruins, and no tillage in the fields. Every practice that prevailed in Gaeldom has been altered, and become so unnatural in the places that were hospitable."

mì-nàdurra, "unnatural", is the adjective applied to the changes that have overtaken the Gaeltacht, where the ultimately natural language of the Garden of Eden[27]—

> *An labhairt phrìseil chùramach*
> *Rinn cùmhnanta ri Adhamh*
>
> (4034–4035)

"The precious, precise speech that sealed covenants with Adam" – had hitherto survived in its richness and purity. The effectiveness of *Oran nam Balgairean* derives from Donnchadh Bàn's full imaginative realization of the society of his youth, which combined a long literary and musical tradition with an economy, dependent for survival on the skills of the hunter and fisherman – a society which in many ways was still pre-agricultural and heroic. Although his eye for landscape is as keen as Thomson's or Wordsworth's, his concerns are very different. They are not primarily with the picturesque or the sublime. The subject of his most famous ode, Ben Dóbhrain, is beautiful, not simply because it provides good hunting, but for the rather more elaborate reason that the nature of the mountain is to bring the men and animals who provide good hunting to the full height of their natural capacity. His Nature depends on hunting, and extends favourable treatment to hunters and their quarry. This is how he describes the stream from which the hinds drank[28]:—

> *Cha bhiodh ìot' air an teangaidh*
> *Taobh shìos a Mhill Teanail,*
> *Le fion Uillt na h-Annaid,*
>   *Blas meala r'a òl air:*
> *Sruth brìoghmhor geal tana,*
> *'S e sìothladh troimh 'n ghaineamh*
> *'S e 's milse na 'n caineal,*
>   *Cha b' aineolach òirnn e.*
> *Siud an ìocshlainte mhaireann*
> *Thig a ìochdar an talaimh*
> *Gheibhte lìonmhorachd mhaith dhith*
>   *Gun a cheannach le stòras,*
> *Air fàrainn na beinne*
> *As dàicheile sealladh*
> *A dh'fhàs anns a' cheithreamh*
>   *A bheil mi 'n Roinn Eòrpa*
>   (3128–3143)

"Down below Meall Teanail their tongue would not be parched, when there is wine of Annat Burn, honey-flavoured to drink: a potent, bright, limpid stream, filtering through the sand; 'tis sweeter than cinnamon, nor was it unknown to us. That was the never-failing tonic which comes from nether strata: abundant good was derived from it without purchase by riches, within the ben's precincts, where the scene is the fairest that evolved in the quarter of Europe I live in."

The language here operates on two levels. One is purely descriptive. The other – and it is the more common in the poem – juxtaposes and contrasts the age-old life of Ben Dóbhrain with that of the farmers in the glens, and the town-dwellers outside the Highlands altogether, the whole forming the quarter of Europe in which Donnchadh Bàn saw himself as living. The wine of Ben Dóbhrain is the water of the Annat Burn, which itself derives its name and properties from the early Christian chapel site, the *annat*[29], on its banks; the water is sweeter than the exotic Biblical cinnamon, recently made familiar by the East India Company. Like the waters of European spas, it has tonic properties, derived from rock and soil, but the hinds and the hunters have no need to pay money in order to receive the benefits. Donnchadh Bàn more than once refers to Europe in the poem and the effect is to contrast the mountain, where the deer and the hunter "ought" to be, (*Tha'n eilid anns an fhrìth/Mar bu chòir dhi bhith* (2934–2935), "The hind is in the forest, as she ought to be") with the unnatural and inferior life of farmers and city-dwellers. The dress of the forest has beauty without foppishness. (The Macaronis, satirized by Robert Fergusson, have no place on Ben Dóbhrain):—

> 'S aigeannach fear eutrom
> Gun mhórchuis,
> Theid fasanda 'na éideadh
> Neo-sporsail
> (2782–2785)

"Sprightly is the lively one, without vanity, that stylishly puts on his garb, not foppishly."

Tuberculosis and other city diseases are unknown on the mountain:—

> Ged théid i 'na cabhaig
> Cha ghearain i maothan:
> Bha sìnnsireachd fallain.
> (2822–2824)

"Though she be hurried, no chest-complaint ails her – her forebears were healthy."

Sight is clear and piercing:—

> Plosg-shùil mheallach gheur
> Gun bhonn glòinin innt',
> Rosg fo mhala léith
> Cumail seòil oirre
> (2918–2921)

"His flashing, soft, sharp eye has no trace of cast in it; eyelid below grey eyebrow is controlling it."

The hind will have nothing to do with the coarse grass eaten by the black cattle who provided food for the English market:—

> Mu Làrach na Féinne
> 'Sa' Chraig Sheilich 'na dhéidh sin,
> Far an cruinnich na h-éildean
>   Bu neo-spéiseil mu'n fhòlach
>   (3116–3119)

"About Larach na Feinne, on Craig Seileach thereafter, where gather the hinds that disdained the rank field grass."

(One should not miss the heroic connotations of the place-name *Làrach na Féinne*, "battle-field of the Fenians", that is "of the followers of Fionn", the Fingal of Macpherson's *Ossian*, discussed below.)

The hind enjoys an almost pre-lapsarian state; she has no need of marriage, and yet has none of the coarseness of a loose woman:—

> Leannan an fhir léith
> As faramaiche ceum,
> Nach iarradh a' chléir
>   A thoirt pòsaidh dhaibh;
> 'S glan fallain a cré
> Is banail i 'na beus,
> Cha robh h-anail breun
>   Ge bè phògadh i.
>   (3188–3195)

"This mistress of the grey lad that has the sprightliest step, and would not request the clergy to marry them. Pure, wholesome is her frame, she is modest in her style, nor was her breath offensive, if one caressed her."

Old age has no burdens:—

> An aois cha chuir truim' orra,
> Mulad no mìghean
>   (2858–2859)

"Age brings them no burden, gloom or dejection."

Only death without Christian hope remains a terror:—

> Gun channtaireachd, gun cheilearachd
> Ach dranndail chon a' deileis rith',
> A ceann a chur gu peirealais,
>   Aig eilid Beinne Dòbhrain
>   (3276–3279)

"For the hind of Ben Dóbhrain there is neither chant nor carolling, but snarl of dogs ravening for her, to drive her head to frenzy."

All this is expressed in an elaborate metrical form, based on pibroch, and closely akin to the structure of the Greek choral ode. The effect depends on the contrast, which in turn must derive from Donnchadh Bàn's experiences outside the Highlands, between Ben Dóbhrain on the one hand, and Europe on the other. The poem is the converse of *The Seasons*; a document of the Enlightenment which derives from the dark rather than the bright face of the moon.

iv

Smollett was aware of this side of Scottish life; his spokesman in *Humphry Clinker* is the romantic Jery Melford, nephew of Matthew Bramble. His reactions, however, are conditioned in a way not yet discussed. Donnchadh Bàn makes occasional references to Fionn, Cù Chulainn and other heroes of the Gaelic epic tradition, but it is not from any such source that Jery draws his information[30]:—

> "We have had princely sport in hunting the stag on these mountains – These are the lonely hills of Morven, where Fingal and his heroes enjoyed the same pastime: I feel an enthusiastic pleasure when I survey the brown heath that Ossian wont to tread; and hear the wind whistle through the bending grass – When I enter our landlord's hall, I look for the suspended harp of that divine bard, and listen in hopes of hearing the aerial sound of his respected spirit – The Poems of Ossian are in every mouth."

James Macpherson lived from 1736 to 1796. The bulk of his published creative work appeared in four volumes, *The Highlander* (1758), *Fragments of Ancient Poetry* (1760), *Fingal* (1762) and *Temora* (1763). To these must be added the earlier attempt at extended narrative verse, entitled by Malcolm Laing *The Hunter*, which during Macpherson's lifetime remained unpublished. Macpherson was the author of other poems, but it is upon those mentioned that any critical assessment of his work must be based. The *Fragments*, *Fingal* and *Temora* all appeared as translations from the Gaelic of Ossian son of Fingal, a bard of the third century A.D., who in old age related the heroic exploits of his youth and lamented the changes brought about by the passage of time.

It was the claim that the narratives were translations from an ancient original which at the time raised the greatest enthusiasm and the most bitter controversy. From a distance of more than two centuries, it has become possible to take a dispassionate view. Ossian or Oisín may or may not have existed. If he existed, none of his poems have survived. Macpherson found and translated no manuscripts of such antiquity as he claimed. On the other hand, he did know a substantial number of medieval ballads, attributed in the common Gaelic (not simply Irish) tradition to Ossian, many of which he incorporated or adapted into his prose poems. "He is no *fili* (poet)" it was thought in medieval Ireland, "who does not synchronise and harmonise all the stories."[31]. It is very probable that Macpherson began by attempting to synchronize and harmonize the ballad material at his disposal, perhaps to some extent under the genuine belief that he was restoring the *disjecta membra* of ancient Gaelic epics. In addition, he had other motives. He resented the Union of 1707. He was distressed by the destruction of the Highland way of life which followed the '15 and the '45, and which the Enlightenment had done much to make inevitable. At the same time, in the tradition of the Enlightenment, he wished to preserve as much of the old way of life as was possible. He envied the Gaelic-speakers of Ireland the possession of such detailed and well-constructed works as the *Foras Feasa ar Éirinn*[32] (*History of Ireland*) by Geoffrey Keating (*c.* 1570–1646). The final impulse, it is clear, was provided by his own creative urge and philosophic and antiquarian interests.

All Macpherson's significant work belongs to his early manhood and exhibits a remarkably consistent development. From the beginning his concern was with natural man and the expression of natural feeling, as the terms were understood in the middle eighteenth century. For both, he found types – the Hunter, the Highlander, Fingal or Ossian – in the life and traditions of the Gaelic-speaking world[33]. "Send thou the night away in song; and give the joy of grief. For many heroes and maids of love, have moved on Inis-fail: And lovely are the songs of woe, that are heard in Albion's rocks; when the noise of the chace is past, and the streams of Cona answer to the voice of Ossian". Love, war, the hunt, each pursued with a melancholy exuberance of feeling and a natural refinement which lacks all urbanity, mark the natural man or woman as portrayed by Macpherson. Aurelia, for instance, in *The Highlander*[34], is only the first heroine compelled by the natural passion of love to step outside her conventional role and become a warrior:—

> Fate was unkind: just as the lovers wed,
> Nor yet had tasted of the nuptial bed;
> Great Sueno's trumpet called the youth to war,
> He sighed, embraced, and left the weeping fair.
> With love emboldened, up the virgin rose,

> From her soft breast the native woman throws;
> And with the gallant warrior clothes the wife,
> Following her Haco to the bloody strife.
>
> (III.223–230)

Epic rather than ode or pastoral was the natural literary form for such a presentation of natural man. Laing in his commentary again and again notes echoes of Homer, Virgil, Milton, Thomson, the Old Testament, which for him, writing in the nineteenth century, disprove Macpherson's claim to be a translator. For Macpherson in the eighteenth century a reply would have been easy, and indeed was more than once provided, both by himself[35], and by such writers as Hugh Blair in his *Critical Dissertation on the Poems of Ossian, the Son of Fingal* (1763). Epic, the defence runs, is a natural poetic form which Homer, the Old Testament authors and Ossian used by the light of nature. Such later poets as Virgil, Milton and Thomson used it, partly by the light of nature, partly as the result of education and conscious poetic imitation. Inevitably striking resemblances unite the works of the natural epic poets and those of their successors, but in the works of Ossian the resemblances were to be attributed to Nature rather than to imitation or derivation.

Here is Macpherson's own formulation, as it appears in the preface to *Temora*[36]:—

> "The title of Epic was imposed on the poem by myself. The technical terms of criticism were totally unknown to Ossian. Born in a distant age, and in a country remote from the seats of learning, his knowledge did not extend to Greek and Roman literature. If, therefore, in the form of his poems, and in several passages of his diction, he resembles Homer, the similarity must proceed from nature, the original from which both drew their ideas. — — — Though this poem of Ossian has not, perhaps, all the *minutiae* which Aristotle from Homer lays down as necessary to the conduct of an epic poem, yet, it is presumed, it has all the grand essentials of the epopoea. Unity of time, place and action, is preserved throughout. The poem opens in the midst of things; what is necessary of preceding transactions to be known is introduced by episodes afterwards; not formally brought in, but seemingly rising immediately from the situation of affairs. The circumstances are grand, and the diction animated; neither descending into a cold meanness, nor swelling into ridiculous bombast."

The doctrine is an early formulation of ideas on oral literature which have a genuine validity as developed in the work of such modern scholars as H. M. and N. K. Chadwick[37] and A. B. Lord[38], ideas which in fact possess a striking relevance to Gaelic Oral literature.

Professor Thomson has commented[39] that "the lack of architectonic power which Arnold attributed, with some justice, to the Celts, and particularly to Ossian, may be attributed to Macpherson also". Be this as it may, the structure of Macpherson's longer pieces at once becomes clearer, if one bears in mind his formal, epic intentions, and in particular his liberal use of "episodes – – – not formally brought in, but seemingly rising immediately from the situation of affairs"[40]. Macpherson may well have thought that in Gaelic epic it was appropriate for episodes to be more abruptly introduced than in Homer. With the advantage of hindsight, it is possible for us now to compare the abrupt technique found in *Beowulf*, a poem with which Macpherson can have had no acquaintance. Certainly a comparison of the earlier narratives with the later reveals a growing and impressive control over structure and tone.

The Hunter is juvenile throughout, most of all perhaps in the disorder of its narrative and the confused presentation of the natural and supernatural orders. The poem is possibly a first draft of *The Highlander*. The greater control here exhibited, Macpherson achieved by the imposition of a semi-historical framework, probably derived from George Buchanan's *Rerum Scoticarum Historia* (1582), of which Ruddiman's impressive edition had appeared in 1715. The anonymous titular hero of the poem is eventually revealed as Buchanan's 78th Scottish king, Duffus, lost son of the 76th king, Milcolumbus, and eventual successor of the 77th, Indulfus, brother of Milcolumbus. Culena, the name of the heroine, is derived from Culenus, in Buchanan the name of Indulfus's son. The major incidents of the poem also derive from Buchanan. This semi-historical framework is appropriate for epic, and exercised precisely the light control which enabled Macpherson's imagination to work most freely and purposefully. It was a comparatively short step from the partially legendary traditional history of Scotland to the wholly legendary material of the Fenian cycle. Even here, Macpherson attempts with some success to fit all his narratives into a single consistent historical frame. The final product in some ways resembles the well documented imaginary world of J. R. R. Tolkien's *Lord of the Rings*. Directly or indirectly, Tolkien owes a good deal to Macpherson.

The Highlander[41] is linked to the earlier eighteenth century by verse form and traditional poetic diction:—

> Thus said the king. Their willing hands they join,
> The rev'rend priest runs o'er the rites divine.
> The solemn ceremony closed with pray'r,

And Duffus called his own the royal fair.
The storm is ceased; the clouds together fly,
And clear at once the azure fields of sky;
The mid-day sun pours down his sultry flame,
And the wet heath waves glist'ring in the beam.

(VI.141–148)

Even here, however, the last line reveals a sensibility, not typically Augustan – as indeed the entire concept of a heroic poem on events of tenth century Scottish history is not typically Augustan:—

Within the royal hall the nobles sat;
The royal hall in simple nature great.
No pigmy art, with little mimicry,
Distracts the sense, or pains the weary eye:
Shields, spears, and helms, in beauteous order shone.
Along the walls of uncemented stone.

(III.195–200)

Almost inevitably, Macpherson's concern with simple nature led him away from the pigmy art of the couplet to the longer prose cadences of his *Ossian*[42]:—

"Arise, winds of autumn, arise; blow along the heath!
streams of the mountains roar! roar tempests, in the groves of
my oaks! walk through broken clouds, O moon! show thy pale
face at intervals! bring to my mind the night, when all my
children fell; when Arindal the mighty fell; when Daura the
lovely failed!"

Long cadences and vast emotions alike are controlled and given shape by the consistent imaginary world to which I have already referred, the world which Macpherson constructed from the ballads and from the chronology of the Irish historians. Buchanan's *Historia* had come to seem unsatisfactory, not least because it followed the tradition which assigned the origin of the Scots to Ireland, and which Macpherson entirely repudiated. In his later view, Britain was the starting point from which Ireland had been colonized in two main invasions, the first, that of the Firbolg or Belgae, from southern Britain to southern Ireland, the second and more successful, that of the Caël, Gael, or Caledonians, from northern Britain to northern Ireland. The Caledonians thereafter held the natural sovereignty of Ireland, but were constantly troubled by insurrections of the subject Firbolg, from which time and again they were rescued by the intervention of their kindred from the Scottish highlands and islands. Macpherson was thus able to reconcile the fact that the scene of Fenian romance is in general Ireland with his own assumption that Fingal was a Caledonian from Morven in Argyll. The details of the historical scheme are set out in *A Dissertation concerning the AEra of Ossian* and *A Dissertation concerning the Poems of Ossian*, two of Macpherson's critical and scholarly prefaces, which Laing excluded from his edition.

It is to natural man however that any discussion of Macpherson's work inevitably returns. The entire historical scheme was invented and adapted simply to provide a setting in which the creatures of Macpherson's imagination might appropriately and convincingly flourish. The philosophical, as opposed to the antiquarian, justification of the poems is to be found in the doctrine of the Noble Savage who is more civilized than corrupt urban man. Fingal, Ossian, Cuthullin, Cathmor and the others find their closest kindred in Rousseau's *Émile* (*Émile*, like *Fingal*, appeared in 1762), and Wordsworth's Wanderer, born among the hills of Athol, who

> many an evening, to his distant home
> In solitude returning, saw the hills
> Grow larger in the darkness; all alone
> Beheld the stars come out above his head,
> And travelled through the wood, with no one near
> To whom he might confess the things he saw.
> (*The Excursion* I, 126–131)

NOTES

1. T. Methuen Ward (ed.), *The Poems of Johnson, Goldsmith, Gray, and Collins* (London, 1905), 314–323.
2. Gerald D. Parker (ed.), *John Home Douglas* (Edinburgh, 1972), 35.
3. A. M. Kinghorn and A. Law (eds.), *The Works of Allan Ramsay* IV (S.T.S., Edinburgh and London, 1970), 236.
4. Knapp, *op. cit.*, 233, 237.
5. Knapp, *op. cit.*, 248–249.
6. Knapp, *op. cit.*, 250.
7. D. Forbes (ed.), *An Essay on the History of Civil Society, 1767, by Adam Ferguson LL.D.* (Edinburgh, 1966), 8.
8. Chapter xxiii, A. Lang (ed.), *Rob Roy* (Border edition, London, 1908), 310.
9. E. MacNeill, *Phases of Irish History* (Dublin, 1919), 5ff.
10. J. Carmichael Watson (ed. and transl.), *Gaelic Songs of Mary MacLeod* (London and Glasgow, 1934), 24–25. For Gaelic poetry of the 17th and 18th centuries, see especially D. Thomson, *An Introduction to Gaelic Poetry* (London, 1973), chapters 4 and 5.

11. Annie M. Mackenzie (ed. and transl.), *Orain Iain Luim* (S.G.T.S., Edinburgh, 1964), 84–85.
12. J. C. Watson, *op. cit.*, 28–29.
13. W. Matheson (ed. and transl.), *The Blind Harper* (S.G.T.S., Edinburgh, 1970), 58–73.
14. Mackenzie, *op. cit.*, 188–189.
15. Mackenzie, *op. cit.*, 206–209.
16. A. and A. MacDonald (eds. and transls.), *The Poems of Alexander MacDonald (Mac Mhaighstir Alasdair)* (Inverness, 1924), 8–9.
17. A. and A. MacDonald, *op. cit.*, 118–119.
18. A. and A. MacDonald, *op. cit.*, 272–273.
19. A. and A. MacDonald, *op. cit.*, 24–25.
20. A. and A. MacDonald, *op. cit.*, 30–31. The entire poem occupies 28–35.
21. J. MacQueen, *Allegory* (2nd edit., London, 1976), 35.
22. A. and A. MacDonald, *op. cit.*, 370–401.
23. MacQueen, *Allegory*, 44; Alice Miskimin, "Patterns in *The Kingis Quair* and the *Temple of Glas*", *Papers on Language and Literature* 13 (1977), 339–361; MacQueen, "The Literature of Fifteenth-Century Scotland" in Jennifer M. Brown (ed.), *Scottish Society in the Fifteenth Century* (London, 1977), 189–192, "Neoplatonism and Orphism in Fifteenth-Century Scotland", *Scottish Studies* 20 (1976), 69–89; Miskimin, "The Design of Douglas's *Palice of Honour*", *Actes du 2ᵉ colloque de langue et de litterature ecossaises (moyen age et renaissance)* (Strasbourg, 1979), 396–408.
24. A. MacLeod (ed.), *The Songs of Duncan Ban Macintyre* (S.G.T.S., Edinburgh, 1952), 32–33.
25. "Oran do Iain Caimbeul a' Bhanca", MacLeod, *op. cit.*, 46–47.
26. MacLeod, *op. cit.*, 346–347.
27. "Rann do'n Ghaidhlig 's do'n Phiob-Mhoir 'sa' Bhliadhna 1782" ("Ode to Gaelic and the Great Pipe in the Year 1782"), MacLeod, *op. cit.*, 276–277.
28. MacLeod, *op. cit.*, 214–217. With this account, cf. W. Gillies, "The Poem in Praise of Ben Dobhrain", *Lines Review* 63 (December 1977), 42–48.
29. W. J. Watson, *History of the Celtic Place-names of Scotland* (Edinburgh and London, 1926), 250–251, 436–437.
30. Knapp, *op. cit.*, 240.
31. R. G. Best, O. Bergin, M. A. O'Brien, *The Book of Leinster* (5 vols., Dublin, 1954–1967), IV.837; the statement comes at the end of a list of sagas which the *fili* was required to know. See H. M. and N. K. Chadwick, *The Growth of Literature* I (Cambridge, 1932), 169.
32. D. Comyn and P. S. Dinneen (eds.), *Foras Feasa ar Eirinn* (Irish Texts Society, IV, VIII, IX, XV, Dublin, 1901, 1905, 1906, 1913).
33. M. Laing, *The Poems of Ossian* (Edinburgh, 1805; reprinted, 2 vols., Edinburgh, 1971), I.45–46. The extract is from Book I of *Fingal*.
34. Laing, *op. cit.*, II.552.
35. In *A Dissertation Concerning the AEra of Ossian* and *A Dissertation Concerning the Poems of Ossian*, both of which, together with H. Blair, *A Critical Dissertation on the Poems of Ossian, the Son of Fingal*, appear in volume III of *The Poems of Ossian* (London, 1796).
36. Laing, *op. cit.*, II.6–7.
37. *The Growth of Literature* (3 vols., Cambridge, 1932–1940).

38. *The Singer of Tales* (Cambridge, Mass., 1960).
39. *The Gaelic Sources of Macpherson's 'Ossian'* (Edinburgh and London, 1951), 13.
40. Laing, *op. cit.*, II.7.
41. Laing, *op. cit.*, II.527–583.
42. Laing, *op. cit.*, I.464.

CHAPTER V

SECULAR MAN: Clerk of Penicuik, Smollett, Ramsay and Boswell

Ramsay, Thomson, Smollett and Fergusson were not themselves either improvers or scientists. Donnchadh Bàn and James Macpherson consciously attached themselves to a world which despised such interests. As opposed to all these, Ramsay's friend, Sir John Clerk of Penicuik (1676–1755), achieved much in agriculture and industry, and was fascinated by Newtonian physics. "Amongst all the studies I followed," he remarks in his *Memoirs*[1], "I cou'd have preferred Mathematicks and Phylosophy, but as my Lot was calculated for publick business I was oblidged to follow such Studies as tended to improve me in this way, such as Law, History and political Essays." The *Memoirs* conclude (pp 232–234) with a substantial "List of Improvements made by me at Pennicuike and Mavisbank, likeways at Cammo in the parish of Cramond." Plantations, enclosures and coalmining were his principal concerns, but the range of his interests can be seen in almost any extract from his book. Under the year 1751, for instance, he comments[2]:—

"If all the world were as frugal as by the dictates of good economy they ought to be, the half of Mankind wou'd starve. The poor must always live by the prodigality and extravagances of the Rich, at least every man who can afford to spend a little might do it for the benefite of the poor, and indeed this is the best way I know for bestowing of charity, except it be carried to a hight that must do manifest prejudice to our children and poor Relations who cannot work for their bread.

In 1750 I found myself very ill used by some whom I trusted at Lonhead in the management of my Coal affaires, therefor I put them in the hands of my son James, who had more strength of Body and more leisure to look after them, for in the management of coal I judged that there was a necessity frequently to go below ground, and not to trust those called

96

oversmen, cheques and coalgrives. Besides as to the choise of my son for chief Manadger, there was a necessity to breed him up a little in the management of these matters.

This experiement I found succeeded to my Wishes, for the profits of my coal began to be doubled.''

One may remark in passing that the miners at Loanhead, as everywhere else in Scotland, were at this time still serfs[3]. Clerk takes the fact for granted – his *Memoirs* contain no reference to a status which might have been expected to disgust, or at least distress, him. His failure to comment resembles Smollett's complacency about the slave trade, and lacks even the mildly redeeming irony of Smollett's narrative.

Apart altogether from such considerations, the nice combination of economic theory and practice in the passage quoted would scarcely lead one to expect something like the following, which combines sensibility with considerable astronomical knowledge, and a lingering trace of superstitious feeling, partly rationalized, partly to be explained by hindsight; as the year referred to is 1744. The comet, Clerk is half-inclined to think, might have been a prognostication of the '45[4].

"This year, about the 19 or 20 of feb., I came out to Pennicuik and in a clear fine morning, half an houer before the sun rose, I saw the beautifullest schene in the Heavens that perhaps, ever was seen by anybody at one time, for by the assistance of a Reflecting Telescope I saw first the Comet with its Tail in the greatest glory it had ever appeared, being at that time within a day or two of its perihelion. Next I saw the planet of Venus in great beuty, and towards the west the planets of Saturn and Jupiter with their satellites; but what made the finest appearance of all, was the moon near her last quarter, just going down upon the Top of the black hill north west of Pennicuik House. Next the sun rose in great splendour, which yet for half an houer did not obscure the Comet, for both it and its Tail appeared very finely for that space. I tried at that time to have seen Mercury, which I cou'd not do, but by the Comet's distance from the Sun's body, I was sure that its perihelion wou'd be within the orbite of that planet. All this I saw without either fogs or clouds interveening. If comets presage great alterations and Trubles in states, this comet may be thought a foreruner, and tho' it be a little superstitious to think so, yet I am tempted to think that as the moon in some cases influences our bodies, I know not how far the vapours which arise from a Comet may not have some influence on Men's minds. It is

> certain that before great Calamities hapning to a nation,
> Comets have been seen, hovering in the Aire, and other odd
> phenomena. All Histories are full of such accounts, and
> Josephus takes notice of a very remarkable one befor the
> destruction of Jerusalem."

Clerk admits to what he recognises as superstitious feelings, while at the same time demonstrating (not too convincingly) that scientific justification of these feelings remains at least a possibility. By 1744 the value of Newton's *Principia* had long been recognised, but Clerk's prose still resounds with the excitement which had greeted the demonstration that even comets obeyed the simple laws of motion and universal gravitation.

The sympathy felt by literary men for the new scientific philosophy in itself bears witness to the secular spirit which came to characterize educated Scots of the period. Hume is the most notable, but Thomson, to judge from his poems and from his praise of Shaftesbury, was more deist than orthodox Christian. That Clerk and Ramsay shared something of the same spirit is further demonstrated by the mere fact that, in the context of late seventeenth and early eighteenth century Scottish Presbyterianism, one was a practical improver on the large scale, and the other wrote a play, *The Gentle Shepherd* (1726), in Scots, and even attempted to open a theatre in Edinburgh. (Thomson was more fortunate in having the London stage as an outlet for his dramatic talent which deserves more credit than on the whole it has received.) Clerk's purchase[5] from Ramsay's bookshop of works by Voltaire (the *Henriade* in 1733, *Lettres philosophiques* in 1734) confirms the general impression. Smollet tends to express fairly conventional religious sentiments, but the spirit of his novels is decidedly secular. One recollects, for instance, Lismahago's account to Mrs Tabitha of his captivity among the American Indians[6]:—

> "Then she asked whether his (Indian) consort had been high-church, or low-church, presbyterian or anabaptist, or had been favoured with any glimmering of the new light of the gospel? When he confessed that she and her whole nation were utter strangers to the christian faith, she gazed at him with signs of astonishment, and Humphry Clinker, who chanced to be in the room, uttered a hollow groan.
>
> After some pause, 'In the name of God, captain Lismahago (cried she), what religion do they profess?" As to religion, madam, (answered the lieutenant), it is among those Indians a matter of great simplicity – they never heard of any *Alliance*

between Church and State. – They, in general, worship two
contending principles; one the Fountain of all Good, the
other the source of evil. – The common people there, as in other
countries, run into the absurdities of superstition; but sensible
men pay adoration to a Supreme Being, who created and
sustains the universe.' 'O! what a pity (exclaimed the pious
Tabby), that some holy man has not been inspired to go and
convert these poor heathens!'

The lieutenant told her, that while he resided among them,
two French missionaries arrived, in order to convert them to
the catholic religion; but when they talked of mysteries and
revelations, which they could neither explain nor authenticate,
and called in the evidence of miracles which they believed upon
hearsay; when they taught, that the Supreme Creator of
Heaven and Earth had allowed his only Son, his own equal in
power and glory, to enter the bowels of a woman, to be born as
a human creature, to be insulted, flagellated, and even executed
as a malefactor; when they pretended to create God himself, to
swallow, digest, revive, and multiply him *ad infinitum*, by the
help of a little flour and water, the Indians were shocked at the
impiety of their presumption. – They were examined by the
assembly of the sachems, who desired them to prove the
divinity of their mission by some miracle. – They answered that
it was not in their power. – 'If you really were sent by Heaven
for our conversion (said one of the sachems), you would
certainly have some supernatural endowments, at least you
would have the gift of tongues, in order to explain your
doctrine to the different nations among which you are
employed; but you are so ignorant of our language, that you
cannot express yourselves even on the most trifling subjects.'

In a word, the assembly were convinced of their being cheats,
and even suspected them of being spies: – they ordered them a
bag of Indian corn a-piece, and appointed a guide to conduct
them to the frontiers; but the missionaries having more zeal
than discretion, refused to quit the vineyard. – They persisted in
saying mass, in preaching, baptizing, and squabbling with the
conjurers, or priests of the country, till they had thrown the
whole community into confusion. – Then the assembly
proceeded to try them as impious impostors, who represented
the Almighty as a trifling, weak, capricious being, and
pretended to make, unmake, and reproduce him at pleasure:

they were, therefore, convicted of blasphemy and sedition, and condemned to the stake, where they died singing *Salve regina*, in a rapture of joy, for the crown of martyrdom which they had thus obtained.

In the course of this conversation, lieutenant Lismahago dropt some hints by which it appeared he himself was a freethinker. Our aunt seemed to be startled at certain sarcasms he threw out against the creed of St. Athanasius. — He dwelt much upon the words *reason, philosophy*, and *contradiction in terms* — he bid defiance to the eternity of hell fire; and even threw such squibs at the immortality of the soul, as singed a little the whiskers of Mrs. Tabitha's faith; for, by this time, she began to look upon Lismahago as a prodigy of learning and sagacity."

Lismahago's opinions generally stand in close comic relationship with those of Smollett himself, and it is probable that here also the two are very close. Smollett pretends that the attack is confined to Roman Catholicism but the turn of the passage, and the tone even before the missionaries are introduced, makes it plain that all forms of Christian worship and theology lie open to similar attack. Enlightenment belongs more to the sensible men among the Red Indians than to the majority of Smollett's European contemporaries.

Most of the authors mentioned reacted in a marked degree against the religious enthusiasm of the Covènanters and Cameronians of the seventeenth century, a reaction which naturally received the strongest expression from those who remained in Scotland. "Enthousiastick notions, superstition, and singularity in Religious points are my utter aversion", Clerk observed (p. 216), and Ramsay condems enthusiasm (in the eighteenth century sense of the word) even more decisively[7]:—

> Enthousiastick vile delusion
> which glories in stift-rumpt confusion,
> gives sanction to Rebellious plots,
> and finds out grace in cutting Throats,
> which, in the reigns of James & Charles,
> prompted these Covenanted Quarles
> and heezd the Leaguers up the Ladders
> to swing aloft in hempen Tedders,
> now since the softener of this rage
> the mannerly reforming Stage,
> is tane away, 'tis justly dreaded,
> 'twill be by Biggotry succeeded

> Divisions from Divisions spring,
> and partys spiteful dart the sting
> ("Epistle to Mr H. S. at London Novr. 1738", 77–90)

The closure of the Edinburgh theatre was the triumph of bigotry which made Ramsay anticipate the renewal of the Solemn League and Covenant, and the return of the Killing Times, when the Cameronians declared war on the state. The action of *The Gentle Shepherd* turns on the restoration of the Scottish royal line in 1660, one incidental happy consequence of which was the expulsion of the Whigs to the moors[8]:—

> Things have taken sic a Turn
> Will gar our vile Oppressors stend like Flaes,
> And skulk in Hidlings on the Hether Braes.
> (II.i, 16–18)

The Covenanters cannot thus be dismissed in a single couplet, but the strength of Ramsay's feelings may be judged from the mere fact that he attempted to do so. Indeed, the reaction against Covenanting principles was one of the great formative elements in the Scottish Enlightenment. It is as strong in Hume or Burns as in Ramsay, and it had lost little force even when Scott and Galt disputed the matter in *Old Mortality* and *Ringan Gilhaize*. Each of these opponents, in his different way, achieved a balanced view, but only with the nineteenth century did such views become possible, even for exceptional men like Scott and Galt.

Had they thought in such terms, Ramsay and his contemporaries would probably have emphasized only the negative contribution of the Covenanters to the secular ideals and material prosperity of the Enlightenment. By the early nineteenth century, a more positive view had also begun to emerge. I have already mentioned, for instance, the portrayal of Davie Deans, the dour but intelligent and, in his way, adaptable Cameronian farmer in Scott's *Heart of Midlothian*, with which may be compared the presentation of Claude Walkinshaw, the superstitious pedlar who becomes a successful Glasgow business man, in Galt's *The Entail*. Neither is an attractive figure, but similar men contributed largely to the establishment, and, by way of descendants who inherited their wealth, to the continuance of Enlightenment society in Scotland. Both represent aspects of the development of a secular capitalist economy on the basis of Protestant, and in particular Calvinistic, ethics, the classic study of which is R. H. Tawney's *Religion and the Rise of Capitalism*. The theme will often recur in the course of these volumes, but for the present it is enough to observe that Ramsay's biblical, prophetic tone when he contemplates the prospect of plenty, or Thomson's when he praises British colonial or mercantile enterprise, are equally results of what Tawney called[9] "The Triumph of the Economic Virtues" and "The New Medicine for Poverty". The Cameronians took possession of society when it became possible to identify predestination to salvation with national progress and individual prosperity. For most Scots, Holy Willie became a particularly uncomfortable acquaintance, because his hypocrisy stood so close to the most rational and enlightened virtues of his century[10]:—

> But, L — — d, remember me and mine
> Wi' mercies temporal and divine!
> That I for grace and gear may shine,
>   Excell'd by nane!
> And a' the glory shall be thine!
>   Amen! Amen!
>   (97–102)

ii

As the eighteenth century advanced, a moderate secularism became increasingly characteristic of prosperous people, whether or not they maintained external allegiance to the tradition of the Covenant. In literature and the arts, this secularism found a convenient, because semi-disguised, expression in classicism. The disguise was sometimes easy to penetrate. If Galt's *The Entail*, for instance, is to be trusted, the classical architecture of St. Andrew's Church — virtually the first in Glasgow to be built (1739–1756) since the Reformation — readily revealed its inward meaning to the eye of the godly. Here is a conversation between Claude Walkinshaw and Cornelius Luke, the tailor, who was an elder of the Gothic and orthodox Tron Kirk (in pre-Reformation times, the collegiate church of St. Mary and St. Anne)[11]:—

> " 'Come your ways, Cornie,' said the intending lover; 'I want to speak to you, anent what's doing about the new kirk on the Green Know.'
> 'Doing, Mr Walkinshaw! – it's a doing that our bairns' bairns will ne'er hear the end o' – a rank and carnal innovation on the spirit o' the Kirk o' Scotland,' replied the elder – 'It's to be after the fashion o' some prelatic Babel in Lon'on, and they hae christened it already by the papistical name o' St Andrew – a sore thing that, Mr Walkinshaw; but the Lord has set his face against it, and the builders thereof are smitten as wi' a confusion o' tongues, in the lack o' siller to fulfil their idolatrous intents – Blessed be His name for evermore! But was no Mr Kilfuddy, wha preached for Mr Anderson last Sabbath, most sweet and

delectable on the vanities of this life, in his forenoon lecture?
and did na ye think, when he spoke o' that seventh wonder o'
the world, the temple of Diana, and enlarged wi' sic pith and
marrow on the idolaters in Ephesus, that he was looking o'er his
shouther at Lowrie Dinwiddie and Provost Aiton, who are no
wrangt in being wytid wi' the sin o' this inordinate super-
structure? – Mr Walkinshaw, am nae prophet, as ye will ken,
but I can see that the day's no far aff, when mininsters of the
gospel in Glasgow will be seen chambering and wantoning to
the sound o' the kist fu' o' whistles, wi' the seven-headed beast
routing its choruses at every o'ercome o' the spring."

A revival of Catholicism or Episcopalianism is only the disguise for
what Cornelius really feels; that the order and symmetry of the new
building in some way threatens the beliefs of his own upbringing. His
fears find appropriate images in classical mythology, dancing, music and
love-making; everything which his enemies considered gracious and
refined. It is an additional irony that the outburst is addressed to the
genuinely carnal Walkinshaw, who uses it to benefit himself by obtain-
ing from Cornelius a new coat at the cheapest possible price.

Distaste for enthusiasm as it had existed in the near past, and still to
some measure survived in such people as Cornelius, merged into a dislike
of Gothic architecture and literature, the characteristic forms of the
enthusiastic and therefore barbarous past, and produced a new devotion
to the balance and restraint of the Greek and Roman world.
Architecture, as Galt indicates, revealed the new trend most clearly, with
Robert Adam (1728–1792) as the most distinguished individual architect,
and the New Town of Edinburgh as the most extended native example.
At an earlier date, Sir John Clerk had combined architecture with
literature in his mansion completed in 1724 at Mavisbank in Midlothian.
The design was his own[12], "under the correction of one Mr Adams, a
skilful architect" (p. 115) – William Adam (died 1748), that is to say,
father of the more celebrated Robert and his brothers. The classical
design of the house is emphasised by the two Latin inscriptions, one in
verse, the other in prose, which adorn the front[13]. Indeed, one set of
phrases from the prose inscription – *non magnificam, non superbam, at
qualem vides, commodam, mundam, genialem* – is as much an epigraph for the
new movement as for the house.

Ramsay's imitations of Horace attempt the most thorough amalgama-
tion of vernacular literature with classical ideals. It is a mistake to regard
them as primarily translations; they are imitations in the full eighteenth
century sense of the word. In Pope's *Imitations of Horace*, John Butt has

remarked[14], "the words of Horace are translated and applied to modern conditions, and thus the weight of Roman satiric tradition is enlisted in the fight against modern corruption." Ramsay's imitations have the same function in relation to the ethnics and customs of Scottish society. That society was still predominantly Calvinistic and for a poet who wished to alter it, or at least to mock it, an effective instrument was provided by the more Epicurean among the *Odes* of Horace. Like Horace, Ramsay might have described himself as *parcus deorum cultor* and *Epicuri de grege porcum*; the effectiveness of his indirect attack may be judged by a comparison of the adaptation of *Solvitur acris hiems* (I.iv), which he published in 1721 as "An Ode to Mr F."[15]:—

> O kanny F————! Tutor Time,
> And live as lang's ye'r in your Prime;
> That ill bred Death has nae Regard
> To King or Cottar, or a Laird,
> As soon a Castle he'll attack,
> As Waus of Divots roof'd wi' Thack.
> Immediately we'll a' take Flight
> Unto the mirk Realms of Night,
> As Stories gang, with Gaists to roam,
> In gloumie *Pluto's* gousty Dome;
> Bid fair Good-day to Pleasure syne
> Of bonny Lasses and red Wine.
>   Then deem ilk little Care a Crime,
> Dares waste an Hour of precious Time;
> And since our Life's sae unko short,
> Enjoy it a', ye've nae mair for't.
>
> (25–40)

with a fairly typical passage from Thomas Boston's lastingly influential *Human Nature in its Fourfold State of Primitive Integrity, Entire Depravity, Begun Recovery and Consummate Happiness or Misery*, published in 1720[16]:—

> "*Thirdly*, Employ yourselves in weaning your hearts from the world. The man who is making ready to go abroad, busies himself in taking leave of his friends. Let the mantle of earthly enjoyments hang loose about you; that it may be easily dropped, when death comes to carry you away into another world. Moderate your affections towards your lawful comforts of life: let not your hearts be too much taken with them. The traveller acts unwisely, who suffers himself to be so allured with

the conveniences of the inn where he lodges, as to make his necessary departure from it grievous. Feed with fear, and walk through the world as pilgrims and strangers. The same as, when the corn is forsaking the ground, it is ready for the sickle; when the fruit is ripe, it falls off the tree easily; so when a Christian's heart is truly weaned from the world, he is prepared for death, and it will be the more easy to him. A heart disengaged from the world is a heavenly one: we are ready for heaven when our heart is there before us, Matt.vi.21."

One may well find Boston, at least in this passage, more attractive than Ramsay. At the same time, it is easy to see the enormous possibility of destructive hypocrisy in a society where Boston's ideals were given too ready lip-service. So too, Boston's detachment from the world entails also that he willingly accepts consummate misery as the appropriate fate for many in the world to come, a misery which he visualises with pitiless accuracy[17]:—

"But they shall be miserable beyond expression, in a relative separation from God. Though he will be present in the very centre of their souls, if I may so express it, while they are wrapt up in fiery flames, in utter darkness; it shall only be to feed them with the vinegar of his wrath, and to punish them with the emanations of his revenging justice: they shall never more taste of his goodness and bounty, nor have the least glimpse of hope from him. They will see his heart to be absolutely alienated from them, and that it cannot be towards them; that they are the party against whom the Lord will have indignation for ever. They shall be deprived of the glorious presence and enjoyment of God; they shall have no part in the beatific vision; nor see any thing in God towards them, but one wave of wrath rolling after another."

By contrast, Ramsay's jauntily sceptical "As Stories gang, with Gaists to roam" seems even now the voice of common sense, and in early eighteenth century Scotland the effect must have been almost exhilarating.

iii

In any discussion of the Scottish Enlightenment, Boston, as chief representative of the opposition, must figure on a scale almost comparable to that appropriate for Hume and Montesquieu. Moral and natural philosophy, the study of human nature in itself and in relation to the environment, rural and urban improvement, secularism and classicism in literature and the arts — all were certainly to be found in eighteenth century Scotland. They cannot, however, be isolated from a background which consisted largely of their opposites. Boston's *Human Nature*, for instance, had a greater immediate effect than Hume's *Treatise*. And so also with more mundane matters. Farming underwent improvement, but even at present on the Scottish mainland conservatism has preserved one or two examples of run-rig; in the eighteenth and early nineteenth century its survival was almost commonplace. These particular contrasts of new and old blended with the other oppositions which had shaped Scottish society from time immemorial – that of Scot and Englishman; Lowlander and Highlander; Scots-speaker, Gaelic-speaker and English-speaker; Calvinist, Episcopalian and Roman Catholic. In Scotland, a simplicity almost patriarchal and a superstitious theocracy survived in immediate contact with the high reaches of European cultivation. Parallel survivals were to be found in many parts of Europe, but nowhere, perhaps, in such concentration, or combined with a University system accessible to a comparatively large section of the population, which thus became familiar with such ideas as those of Hume, Smith, and Montesquieu. Smollett observes[18] that he made Roderick Random a North Briton because "I could at a small expense bestow on him such education as I thought the dignity of his birth and character required, which could not possibly be obtained in England, by such slender means as the nature of my plan would afford. In the next place, I could represent simplicity of manners in a remote part of the kingdom". These words, I am almost tempted to say, embody the essence of the Scottish Enlightenment, the reconciliation of apparent opposites achieved by the greatest philosophic and imaginative writers of the period.

Contrasts in society were a frequent topic of conversation among Scots when James Boswell (1740–1795) visited London in 1762. On Tuesday 23rd November, for instance, he observed[19], "we talked on a rude and on a polished state of society." The same conversation is reported in more detail under Monday 29th November[20]:—

> "Lord Eglinton said that a savage had as much pleasure in eating his rude meals and hearing the rough notes of the bagpipe as a man in polished society had in the most elegant entertainment and in hearing the finest music. Mr Mylne very justly observed that to judge of their happiness we must have the decision of a being superior to them both, who should feel the pleasure of each; and in that case it would be found that although each had his taste fully gratified, yet that the civilized man, having his taste more refined and susceptible of higher enjoyment, must be acknowledged to have the greatest happiness."

Lord Eglinton and Mr Mylne were both Scots, and obviously based their discussion not so much on the voyages and discoveries of the time as on their own contrasting experiences of Highland, Lowland and English society. The ideas are little more than commonplace, but bear some relationship to more developed investigations such as Adam Ferguson's *An Essay on the History of Civil Society*, published five years after the conversation recorded by Boswell. Ferguson's own background, in turn, serves to explain at least something of his choice of subject: he was born in Perthshire with Gaelic as his mother tongue; in addition to his experiences in the Universities of St Andrews and Edinburgh, and in the Advocates' Library, he held from 1745 to 1754 a chaplaincy in the Black Watch, and with his regiment was present at the Battle of Fontenoy in 1745. As Duncan Forbes remarks[21], "Behind the *Essay* lies a deeply felt experience of the contrast between these two societies, (the Highland and the Lowland) and the question: what happens to man in the progress of society?"

The experience might be developed in either of two ways: as with Ferguson, in the direction of sociology and philosophical history, a direction also followed, in their different fashions, by Hume, Smith and Robertson. The alternative was a concern for the individual in relation to different societies, as may be illustrated by Smollett, with his narratives of a Scot at large in England, Europe and the world generally, or of a Welsh family at large in England and Scotland. Similar motives led Boswell with Dr Johnson to the Hebrides[22] "with a notion that we might there contemplate a system of life almost totally different from what we had been accustomed to see; and to find simplicity and wildness, and all the circumstances of remote time and place, so near to our native great island."

Boswell most obviously reveals the concern for the individual as the product of a particular society in relation to that and other societies. In the *Journals* he is scientifically concerned with James Boswell, the Edinburgh advocate, son of a Presbyterian judge, affected by the sophistication of England and Europe and their more colourful forms of worship, but equally by the relative simplicities of Corsica, the Hebrides and the Scottish criminal courts. He is himself the object of his scientific enquiries[23]:—

> "The ancient philosopher, certainly gave a wise counsel
> when he said, 'Know thyself'. For surely this knowledge is of all
> the most important — — — A man cannot know himself better
> than by attending to the feelings of his heart and to his external
> actions, from which he may with tolerable certainty judge

'what manner of person he is.' I have therefore determined to
keep a daily journal in which I shall set down my various
sentiments and my various conduct – – – I shall here put down
my thoughts on different subjects at different times, the whims
that may seize me and the sallies of my luxuriant imagination. I
shall mark the anecdotes and the stories that I hear, the
instructive or amusing conversations that I am present at, and
the various adventures that I may have."

Even from this, however, it is clear that Boswell aimed at something
more than self-knowledge. The emphasis on anecdotes, stories and con-
versations show the parallel wish to know others. His concern, like
Hume's, is with human nature generally, and like Montesquieu or
Ferguson, he wishes to analyze human nature in terms of human society.
As a consequence, he came to concentrate on two main objects, the Scot,
James Boswell, and the archetypical product of another society, the
Englishman, Samuel Johnson. (His interest in Rousseau and Voltaire was
similarly motivated). On both he was prepared to use the experimental
method, which sometimes involved, as he himself admitted, treating the
objects of his experiments, even Samuel Johnson, like children[24]:—

"He was indeed, If I may be allowed the phrase, at bottom
much of a *John Bull*, much of a *true-born Englishman*. There was a
stratum of common clay under the rock of marble. – He was
voraciously fond of good eating, and he had a great deal of that
quality called *humour*, which gives an oiliness and a gloss to
every other quality.

I am, I flatter myself, completely a citizen of the world. In my
travels through Holland, Germany, Switzerland, Italy,
Corsica, France, I never felt myself from home; and I sincerely
love 'every kindred and tongue and people and nation.' I
subscribe to what my late truly learned and philosophical friend
Mr Crosbie said: that the English are better animals than the
Scots; they are nearer the sun, their blood is richer and more
mellow; but when I humour any of them in an outrageous
contempt of Scotland, I fairly own I treat them as children. And
thus I have, at some moments, found myself obliged to treat
even Dr Johnson."

Boswell might use such methods occasionally, but never to the neglect
of more conventional laborious and scientific methods of enquiry. The
following paragraph refers to *The Life of Dr Johnson*, but has an obvious
relevance to the *Journals*, and indeed to all his anthropological
studies[25]:—

"The labour and anxious attention with which I have

collected and arranged the materials of which these volumes are
composed, will hardly be conceived by those who read them
with careless facility. The stretch of mind and prompt assiduity
by which so many conversations were preserved, I myself, at
some distance of time, contemplate with wonder; and I must be
allowed to suggest, that the nature of the work, in other
respects, as it consists of innumerable detached particulars, all
which, even the most minute, I have spared no pains to ascertain
with a scrupulous authenticity, has occasioned a degree of
trouble far beyond that of any other species of composition.
Were I to detail the books which I have consulted, and the
inquiries which I have found it necessary to make by various
channels, I should probably be thought ridiculously
ostentatious."

The consequence of such labours was that Boswell's portrait of
Johnson is much more than the caricature which the earlier description
of him as a John Bull might have led one to expect. Boswell investigates
every aspect of his subject's personality: the constitutional indolence and
compulsive industry, the religious devotion and the fear of damnation,
the physical peculiarities, the need of male and female companionship.
The Life of Dr Johnson (and the *Journals*) might almost be regarded as an
applied version of Hume's more theoretical *Treatise*.

Boswell stands apart from most of the writers already mentioned in
that agricultural and industrial improvement meant almost nothing to
him. His concern for social anthropology, however, and the intricacies of
the human mind, is typical of the entire Scottish Enlightenment. Boswell
indeed cannot be properly understood save in the context of the Scottish
life and thought of the eighteenth century. His works, including the
great *Life*, belong to Scottish rather than to English letters. He sym-
bolized his allegiance to the central Scottish tradition by the ritual which
accompanied his departure from Edinburgh for London in 1762[26]:—

"I made the chaise stop at the foot of the Canongate; asked
pardon of Mr Stewart for a minute; walked to the Abbey of
Holyroodhouse, went round the Piazzas, bowed thrice: once to
the Palace itself, once to the crown of Scotland above the gate
in front, and once to the venerable old Chapel. I next stood in
the court before the Palace, and bowed thrice to Arthur Seat,
that lofty romantic mountain on which I have so often strayed
in my days of youth, indulged meditation and felt the raptures
of a soul filled with ideas of the magnificence of GOD and his

creation. Having thus gratified my agreeable whim and superstitious humour, I felt a warm glow of satisfaction."

NOTES

1. J. M. Gray (ed.), *Memoirs of the Life of Sir John Clerk of Penicuik, Baronet* (S.H.S., Edinburgh, 1892), 214.
2. Gray, *op. cit.*, 225.
3. W. Ferguson, *Scotland 1689 to the Present* (Edinburgh, 1968), 93, 187–189.
4. Gray, *op. cit.*, 167–168. It is curious that in this passage Clerk seems to hesitate between the pre-Tycho belief that comets were a phenomenon of the upper atmosphere, and the later one that they belonged to interplanetary space.
5. Kinghorn and Law, *op. cit.*, 193, 202.
6. Knapp, *op. cit.*, 195–197.
7. Kinghorn and Law (eds.), *The Works of Allan Ramsay* III (S.T.S., Edinburgh and London, 1961), 249.
8. Burns Martin and J. W. Oliver (eds.), *The Works of Allan Ramsay* II (S.T.S., Edinburgh and London, 1953), 225.
9. These are the titles of sections iii and iv of chapter 4, "The Puritan Movement", in R. H. Tawney's *Religion and the Rise of Capitalism* (Pelican edit., London, 1938 and often reprinted). See also the studies and extracts in M. J. Kitch (ed.), *Capitalism and the Reformation* (London, 1967).
10. J. Kinsley (ed.), *The Poems and Songs of Robert Burns* (3 vols., Oxford, 1968), I.78., (referred to hereafter as Kinsley *Burns*).
11. I. A. Gordon (ed.), *The Entail* (London, 1970), 13–14.
12. Gray, *op. cit.*, 115.
13. Gray, *op. cit.*, 249.
14. *The Augustan Age* (London, 1950), 67.
15. Martin and Oliver (eds.), *The Works of Allan Ramsay* I (S.T.S., Edinburgh and London, 1945), 222.
16. I have used an undated Inverness edition. The passage is from Part IV, "The Eternal State", Section II, "Difference between the Righteous and the Wicked in their Death".
17. Part IV, Section VI, "Of Hell".
18. G. Saintsbury (ed.), *The Adventures of Roderick Random by Tobias Smollett* (3 vols., London, n.d.), I.xlii.
19. F. A. Pottle (ed.), *Boswell's London Journal 1762–1763* (London, 1950), 48.
20. Pottle, *op. cit.*, 56.
21. Forbes, *op. cit.*, xxxix.
22. F. A. Pottle and C. H. Bennett, *Boswell's Journal of a Tour to the Hebrides with Samuel Johnson, LL.D., 1773* (London, 1963), 3.
23. Pottle, *op. cit.*, 39.
24. Pottle and Bennett, *op. cit.*, 10.
25. *Boswell's Life of Johnson* (2 vols., Everyman's Library, London, 1949), xviii.
26. Pottle, *op. cit.*, 41–42.

CHAPTER VI

UNENLIGHTENED AND EARLY DARKENED: Alexander Ross and Robert Fergusson

The first two chapters of this book have shown, among other things how unsatisfactory it is to assume that the language, in particular Scots or English, of eighteenth century Scottish poetry serves as a precise indicator of the social and intellectual expectations of the audience. It is impossible, in other words, to give more than a very limited agreement to statements like that of J. H. Millar[1], "to excel in the use of English and to eschew the Scots dialect became the mark of an enlightened mind and a cultivated taste." The remark applies only to expository prose; Scots poetry was in many ways, primarily intended to satisfy the expectations and presuppositions of readers whose minds were enlightened and whose tastes were cultivated. Many of the *literati* at least tried their hand at composition in Scots, often with some success. Yet Millar's doctrine, in its most absolute form, still persists. One side, taken to the extreme, is exemplified by Mr M. P. McDiarmid's comment[2] that "Modern Scots poetry begins in the seventeenth century as a literary joke"; another by Dr Craig's remark in the introduction to his influential, but often misleading book, *Scottish Literature and the Scottish People, 1690–1830*[3]:—
"Though David Hume could marvel that we should be the people most distinguished for literature in Europe, all that the famous Golden, or Athenian, age could show for imaginative literature was a very striking dearth."

The type of poem to which Mr McDiarmid refers was already well established as a sub-division of polite literature in the fifteenth century. Dr Craig uses the word "literature" in a sense which only partly corresponds to that used by Hume. He leaves out of consideration authors like Thomson and Smollett, who left Scotland for London. He tends to assume that in Scotland Edinburgh stood in the same dominant relation to literary life as did London to English. Burns in particular obviously did not belong to the Edinburgh scene, and it is perhaps primarily for this reason that Dr Craig tends to separate Scots as a local, from English as an international language, to regard London, the model for Edinburgh Scot, as outwith the ken of other Scots, Scotland itself as outwith the ken of Scots in London, and Gaelic as non-existent. As a consequence of all this, he assumes that nothing written in Scots could be a product of the Golden Age.

Fergusson was an Edinburgh man with an "enlightened" education, which helped to shape his poetry. Because he wrote most of his best poetry in Scots, Dr Craig omits him from his consideration of polite literature. For him as for others, Fergusson, with Burns, is no more than the last fruit of an old tree, the last voice of the old communal culture, his creativeness standing in direct opposition to the imaginative sterility of his Golden Age contemporaries. The poetry which matters is Scottish and unenlightened; the prose is English, enlightened and non-imaginative, and between them there is no common ground.

That Scots poetry might be creative, and yet almost wholly untouched by the Enlightenment, I am prepared to grant. The concession however has little or no application to Fergusson or Burns. The qualities which link them specifically to the Enlightenment appear in strong relief if their work is set beside that of an older poet, Alexander Ross, schoolmaster at Lochlee in Glenesk, Angus. Ross lived from 1699 to 1784, and his best-known poem, *The Fortunate Shepherdess, a Pastoral Tale*, first appeared at Aberdeen in 1768, and thereafter was frequently reprinted. Some details of his life might lead one to expect traces of the Enlightenment in his works. He was an Aberdeen graduate, who sometimes attempted serious scholarship, and who was acquainted with some of the *literati*, in particular James Beattie (1735–1803), the opponent of David Hume, and author of *The Minstrel* (1771–1774). *The Fortunate Shepherdess*, indeed, roused Beattie to produce the best verses he ever wrote, "To Mr Alexander Ross at Lochlee, Author of The Fortunate Shepherdess, and other Poems in the Broad Scotch Dialect". The last phrase shows that Beattie did not regard Ross's work as part of polite literature – as in any sense part of the Enlightenment, that is to say – and Beattie's own commendation is unique among his works in that it too is written, not even in Scots, but in a slightly modified Buchan dialect. In the second stanza quoted, for instance, "fustle" = "whistle", with the characteristic local development of "wh" into "f"[4]:—

> Our country leed is far frae barren,
> 'Tis even right pithy and auldfarran.
> Our sells are neiper-like, I warran,
>   For sense and smergh;

In kittle times, when faes are yarring,
   We're no thought ergh.

O bonny are our greensward hows,
Where through the birks the burny rows,
And the bee bums, and the ox lows,
   And saft winds rustle,
And shepherd-lads, on sunny knows,
   Blae the blythe fusle.

'Tis true, we Nordans manna fa'
To eat sae nice, or gang sae bra'
As they that come from far-awa';
   Yet sma's our skaith:
We've peace (and that's well worth it a')
   And meat and claith.

                         (43–60)

Beattie places the emphasis where in one sense it belongs – on the immediacy of contact provided by the poem with a way of life, quite different from the eighteenth century social norm. (In this it bears some resemblance to Donnchadh Bàn's poem on Ben Dobhrain.) He realized too that in some ways the poem is a northern variant of standard eighteenth century pastoral. The vogue for pastoral derives from the optimistic belief in "natural man" and the general benevolence of the Creator and his creation, a belief given alternative expression in, for example, Pope's *Essay on Man*, in the *Profession de foi du vicaire savoyard* which forms the centre piece of Rousseau's *Emile*, and in Burns's "A man's a man for a' that", a belief characteristic of the Enlightenment in Scotland as elsewhere. Schematically, one might say, the poem fits effortlessly into the general pattern of British and European literature of the time, and it is likely that Ross was well aware of the fact.

   Schematically it fits, but not otherwise, and for two reasons. Pastoralism of the English kind demanded that the poet and his audience should remain in some sense detached from the life which he described. The pastoral world is an ideal or an escape; the author and his audience are necessarily outsiders, observers. The characteristic mode is descriptive, with the emphasis on situation rather than story.

   This pattern Ramsay had already broken in *The Gentle Shepherd* by the conscious intrusion of history and realistic geography, as a consequence making his pastoral narrative rather than situational. Macpherson too, it will be remembered, gave a precise, if imaginary, historical background to his more epic style of narrative. To a certain extent Ross follows the same course, but on the whole he fails to see the possibilities of the new form or the necessary conditions governing it. His pastoral is narrative and has a definite geographical setting – the hill-country of Aberdeen-shire and Angus. He is precise on sociological detail, and indeed on every aspect of his narrative connected with the space occupied by the action. He does not, however, realize the importance of historical time – the period and precise historical circumstances of the events depicted in his narrative. His plot does not differ greatly from that of *The Gentle Shepherd*, but the period chosen by Ramsay for his action – Civil War, Commonwealth and Restoration – justifies, at least for stage purposes, some of the improbabilities. In Ross, the lack of similar historic precision makes the plot simply unrealistic and unconvincing, savouring more of New Comedy and Greek romance than of seventeenth or eighteenth century rural Scotland, or even Caledonian antiquity. (The memory of Rob Roy was overnear, perhaps, to enable him to use one possible piece of local detail). The Enlightenment was characterized by an increasingly precise sense of the relationship between historical time and sociological circumstances, substantial traces of which are to be found in Ramsay and Macpherson, but which in Ross is almost entirely lacking. Indeed, the full imaginative expression of the relationship was not reached until Scott and Galt produced their novels in the 'teens and twenties of the nineteenth century.

Ross nevertheless gains something from the form he adopts. Because as a native of Aberdeenshire and schoolmaster of Lochlee he had identified himself with the geographical and sociological world of his characters, and because he was writing for a local audience, he is observant rather than an observer in the main pastoral tradition – he is able, that is to say, to take his landscape for granted, unless some particular feature becomes important for the development of his story. Narrative is always his first concern. The poem contains a good description of a shieling, and shielings, one might think, are of the very stuff from which traditional pastoral is made. (Donnchadh Bàn, it will be recollected, tends to use the shieling as an emblem of the warmth and social relaxation of the older order.) But the vividness of Ross's description is not pastoral nor nostalgic; it arises first from the fact that he was himself as thoroughly familiar with shielings and their function as was his audience; secondly, because the old woman who lives at the shieling is doubly important for the development of his story. She is there to give the Squire information which will enable him to pursue Nory, the fortunate shepherdess, on her return to Flaviana; and later in the poem she has to establish the fact of Nory's aristocratic ancestry. Ross uses some artistry to bring her into contact with the fugitive girls, Nory and Bydhy. They are forced by a thunderstorm to spend a night on the hills; they are cold and wet, and their provisions are exhausted. Naturally, when they see a shieling in the distance, they decide to approach it[5]:—

Sae down they fare, an' rough, rough was the brae,
Wi' craigs an' scrabs a' scatter'd i' the way.
As they drew near, they heard an eldren dey
Singing fu' sweet at milking o' her ky,
In by they come, an' hails'd her cheerfully.
The wife looks up, some little in surprise,
An' leaning o' the boucht the maidens spies,
An' taks hersell, an' says, "Wha have I here?
This day ye seem to be right soon asteer."
Quo they: "We hae ga'en will, an' out a' night,
An' spy'd this sheal, an' came to be set right.
Be but sae kind as tell us where we be,
An' ye's get thanks – 'tis a' we hae to gee."
Quo she: "Unto the sheal step ye o'er by,
An' warm yoursels, till I milk out my ky.
This morning's raw; gin ye've a' night been out,
That ye wad thole a warm I mak na doubt,
An' something mair, I's warrant. Ca' your wa'
The door it stands wide open to the wa'.
Hadd on a cow, till I come o'er the gate,
An' do the best you can to hadd you hett."
The lasses bidding do, an' o'er they gaes,
An' of bleech'd birns put on a canty bleeze.
Content they were at sick a lucky kyle,
An' fand they had na met wi' a beguile.
On skelfs a' round the wa's the cogs were set,
Ready to ream, an' for the cheese be het;
A hake was frae the rigging hinging fu'
Of quarter kebbocks, tightly made an' new.
Behind the door, a calour heather bed,
Flat o' the floor, of stanes an' fail was made.
An' lucky shortly follow'd o'er the gate
Wi' twa fu' leglins, froathing o'er an' het,
Syne ream'd her milk, an' set it o' the fire;
An' bade them eek the bleeze, an' nae to tyre;
That cruds, their weamfu', they sud get on haste,
As fresh an' gueed as ever they did taste

> Sair looked she on Nory's bony face,
> An' says: "Young lass, I wiss you meikle grace.
> Sweet are your looks, an' of gueed nature fu'!
> He'll get nae blind that chances to get you.
> Your bony rozered cheeks an' blinking eyn
> Minds me upon a face I've some time seen."
>
> (2280–2322)

The last words hint, of course, at the final scene of recognition in which Nory's ancestry is brought to light. But here too Ross makes additional provision. The old woman has been the Squire's nurse, and every summer it is his custom to visit her and inspect the shieling. It is thus perfectly natural for him to pay his respects when his pursuit of Nory leads him in that direction. Equally, when he has seen his nurses' fine store of provisions, it is natural for him to call again on his return jouney with his new-won bride. This second visit, in turn, gives the nurse her chance to identify Nory's mother as the child of the Squire's uncle, who long ago had been stolen by gypsies. Nory's marriage to the Squire is thus made socially respectable.

As I have said, the plot of the poem remains romantic and unrealistic. There is, however, nothing specifically romantic about the shieling. A man of the Enlightenment might have treated it in either of two ways; on the one hand, as an interesting antiquarian survival of a regrettably out-moded way of life, or on the other as a relic of barbarism surviving into an age when enclosures and efficient farm management had made shielings and the practice of transhumance unnecessary. For Ross it was neither; a shieling was no more than a shieling, and the details which he supplies are there, not as the result of antiquarian or improving interests, but simply for the sake of the plot.

The final point has already been mentioned. The poem is written, not in the standard literary Scots of Ramsay, Fergusson and Burns, but in the dialect of the north-east. Literary Scots to some small extent prevented Burns, and in a greater measure Ramsay and Fergusson, from gaining an English and European reputation; the Buchan dialect prevented Ross from enjoying even general Scottish esteem. Miss Wattie, in her edition for the Scottish Text Society, listed[6] eighteen earlier editions published between 1768 and 1873; of these, thirteen appeared in Aberdeen, two in Edinburgh, and one each in Glasgow, Dundee and Brechin. Nothing could more plainly establish that the audience for whom the poem had the directest appeal was predominantly local. There is nothing cosmopolitan about Ross.

ii

The contrast with Fergusson is striking, as may most readily be demonstrated by an analysis of one of his best-known poems, *The Farmer's Ingle*. This has received a fair amount of comment, but has not been discussed in every important study of the period. Dr Craig, for one, ignores it; presumably because it is a country poem, while the emphasis in his work lies on the qualities which connect Fergusson with the communal life of pre-Enlightenment Edinburgh. Professor Daiches may be taken as summing up the central critical point of view[7]:—

> "Hitherto Fergusson had excelled as an urban poet, as the bard of Edinburgh, but here he celebrates the agricultural life in a rich, slow-moving verse of a kind that Scottish poetry had not seen for centuries. The stanza is a modified Spenserian; the tone is that of affectionate observation, without a trace of sentimentality; the structure, moving from the vivid description of evening settling over the countryside to the interior domestic scene and then taking the farmer and his family through their evening's activities until they retire to rest, to conclude on a note of peaceful benediction, is perfectly controlled throughout. "The Farmers's Ingle" is a finer poem than Burns's "The Cotter's Saturday Night", which, in spite of some magnificent passages, is confused in tone, motive and diction. Fergusson's very title indicates the superiority: Burns's title sounds as if he is about to show off some model rustics to benevolent genteel observers, whereas Fergusson is describing, with knowledge and affection, what he sees. Here at last is a full-blooded Scots poem, written by the whole man, rich and musical and assured."

"Fergusson is describing what he sees." Well and good – though in parenthesis one may wonder if purely descriptive poetry is ever quite of the first order. Is "one of Fergusson's two real masterpieces" (again to quote Professor Daiches[8]) no better than this? And what *did* Fergusson see? Is the poem merely a series of descriptive sketches? Did Fergusson leave Edinburgh merely to paint a series of *genre* interiors? All these are questions which must present themselves to any serious reader of the poem, and which critics in general have left unanswered. The poem deserves a much closer attention to detail than it has yet, to the best of my knowledge, received.

"The Farmer's Ingle" dates from 1773, a time when agricultural improvement was wide-spread in Scotland, especially in the Lothians. I have already in Chapter I showed Fergussons's awareness of such developments. Yet the system of farming described in "The Farmer's Ingle" is unimproved to a degree so aggressive that it must be intentional. The terms he uses belong to the old world – the farm is a mailing, the farmer a tacksman (with a short lease, one may assume); he operates his farm on the run-rig system (presumably with in-field and out-field), and is thirled to a mill, where the miller takes a multure. His cottage is thatched. He uses oxen to pull the old, clumsy inefficient Scots plough; his threshing is done by flail, and he has no winnowing machine of the type invented by James Meikle in 1710. (Scott in *Old Mortality*, it will be recollected, anachronistically gives even the Covenanting Mause Headrigg an adverse comment on this invention[9]:— "Your leddyship and the steward hae been pleased to propose that my son Cuddie suld work in the barn wi' a new-fangled machine for dighting the corn frae the chaff, thus impiously thwarting the will of Divine Providence, by raising wind for your leddyship's ain particular use by human art, instead of soliciting it by prayer, or waiting patiently for whatever dispensation of wind Providence was pleased to send upon the sheeling-hill."). The fuel burned in the farmer's ingle is peat from the thatched stack on the hill behind the farm: the evening meal consists of ale, bannocks, milk, cream, cheese and kail. The women spin the thread and weave the cloth from which the family's clothing is made; the furniture is obviously primitive, and there is a distinct, but muted, suggestion that at night the farm animals occupy the same building as the farmer and his family.

The one feature which does not fit the old style of farming is the interior cleanliness[10]:—

> The guidman, new come hame, is blyth to find
>   Whan he out o'er the halland flings his e'en,
> That ilka turn is handled to his mind,
>   That a' his housie looks sae cosh and clean;
> For cleanly house loves he, tho' e'er sae mean.
>   (14–18)

"The clartier, the cosier" offers a more accurate summary of the old-fashioned Scottish attitude to home hygiene.

The descriptive parts of the poem, all this is to say, belong essentially to the past rather than to the countryside around Edinburgh which was immediately familiar to Fergusson. Everything in the poem is cosy and secure to a quite unrealistic degree, but the system is still essentially that which in the fifteenth century oppressed the "Maill men, Merchandis and all laboureris", of whom, as Henryson more realistically than Fergusson observed, the life was "half ane Purgatorie"[11]:—

O man but mercie, quhat is in thy thocht,
War than ane Wolf, and thow culd understand?
Thow hes aneuch; the pure husband richt nocht
Bot croip and caff upon ane clout of land.
For Goddis aw, how durst thow tak on hand,
And thow in Barn and Byre sa bene and big,
To put him fra his tak and gar him thig? — —

His Hors, his Meir, he man lend to the Laird,
To drug and draw in Cairt or in Cariage;
His servand or his self may not be spaird
To swing and sweit, withoutin meit or wage.
Thus how he standis in labour and bondage,
That scantlie may he purches by his maill
To leve upon dry breid and watter caill.

Hes thow not reuth to gar thy tennentis sweit
In to thy laubour with faynt and hungrie wame,
And syne hes lytill gude to drink or eit,
With his menye at evin quhen he cummis hame?
(2735–2741, 2749–2759)

Henryson's verse reveals a far greater sensitivity to observed reality than anything in Fergusson's poem.

In the 1770's it would have been impossible for any member of literate Edinburgh society to miss Fergusson's central intention. "The Farmer's Ingle" by its concentration on an idealized and unrealistic past implicity conveys a condemnation, or at least an adverse criticism, of the new order which was rapidly replacing the old, the new order of the Enlightenment and the Improvers. Many of Fergusson's best poems – "On the Death of Scots Music", "The Ghaists", "Hame Content" and "To the Principal and Professors of the University of St Andrews on their superb treat to Dr Samuel Johnson" – turn on some variation of this theme.

Fergusson himself however was never able to make a full resolution of the tension. What should have been the central point of "The Farmer's Ingle" is unfortunately conveyed in the two weakest and most derivative stanzas of the whole poem. Fergusson has been describing the farmer's evening meal:—

Frae this lat gentler gabs a lesson lear;
    Wad they to labouring lend an eidant hand,
They'd rax fell strang upo' the simplest fare,
    Nor find their stamacks ever at a stand.
Fu' hale and healthy wad they pass the day,

At night in calmest slumbers dose fu' sound
Nor doctor need their weary life to spae,
  Nor drogs their noddle and their sense confound,
  Till death slip sleely on, and gie the hindmost wound.

On sicken food has mony a doughty deed
  By Caledonia's ancestors been done;
By this did mony wight fu' weirlike bleed
  In brulzies frae the dawn to set o' sun:
'Twas this that brac'd their gardies, stiff and strang,
  That bent the deidly yew in antient days,
Laid Denmark's daring sons on yird alang,
  Gar'd Scottish thristles bang the Roman bays;
For near our crest their heads they doughtna raise.

                                              (28–45)

Common-place moralizing backed by doubtful history – the contrast
with Henryson is again striking. Fergusson's verse here is only minimally
better than the average of his Scottish Augustan contemporaries, and for
a fairly obvious reason. The reflective movement of the stanza demands a
truth more genuinely universal than Fergusson was able to provide.
What he does offer is at best a half-truth (plain food leads to strength,
long life and national greatness); at worst, a piece of wishful thinking, its
inadequacies mercilessly emphasised by the accomplishment of his
metrical control. Those inadequacies cannot be concealed by a wealth of
Caledonias, antient days, thristles, Danes, Romans and bays derived
from Hector Boece and George Buchanan. Something is rotten in "The
Farmer's Ingle", not least because Fergusson, by ignoring a significant
part of the accomplishment of the Scottish Enlightenment, has tried to
turn poverty and recurrent misery into pastoral and propaganda.

                                              iii
At the same time, it would be a mistake to assume that Fergusson con-
tented himself with a simple laudatory picture of the Scottish past in
every aspect. He was not sufficiently a man of the Enlightenment to
identify himself with the Improvers; he was too much one to be able to
stomach every feature of the older order. I have already commented on
the improbable cleanliness which he imposes on the farmhouse. More
striking is the extent to which the farmer's interests are shown as secular;
there is virtually no hint of the religious and theological obsessions of
seventeenth and eighteenth century rural Scotland – this too despite the
fact that an obsession with theology was held to be a main cause of the
preservation of the older way of life. "An extensive acquaintance with

the mysterious, abstruse and disputed points of systematic divinity, was the species of knowledge they generally sought after, and to which the greatest fame was attached", wrote W. Aiton[12] in his *Agricultural Report on Ayrshire*, and Boston's *Human Nature* was to be found on every farm and cottage shelf. The link with economic stagnation is to be seen in the outburst already quoted, which Scott puts into the mouth of Mause Headrigg. In terms of religion "The Cotter's Saturday Night" is much closer to reality than "The Farmer's Ingle". Burns in other moods and other metres was capable of a very different and secular presentation of the Auld Lichts, but he was also able to give a moving and dignified account of the cottage religion which he had known as a boy[13]:—

> The chearfu' supper done, wi' serious face,
>> They, found the ingle, form a circle wide,
> The sire turns o'er, wi' patriarchal grace,
>> The big ha' Bible, ance his father's pride.
> His bonnet rev'rently is laid aside,
> His lyart haffets wearing thin and bare;
>> Those strains that once did sweet in Zion glide,
> He wales a portion with judicious care,
> And "Let us worship God!" he says, with solemn air.
>
> (100–108)

It is a measure of the range of Burns' intellectual and imaginative power that he was able to write, not only this, but also "The Holy Fair", in which he embodies the very essence of rural religious conservatism, lassitude, and hypocrisy[14]:—

> Now butt an' ben the change-house fills
>> Wi' yill-caup commentators;
> Here's crying out for bakes an' gills,
>> An' there the pint-stowp clatters;
> While thick an' thrang, an' loud an' lang,
>> Wi' logic an' wi' Scripture,
> They raise a din, that in the end
>> Is like to breed a rupture
>> O' wrath that day.
>
> (154–162)

"The Holy Fair" is not such a masterpiece as "Holy Willy's Prayer", but if one compares it with its models, Fergusson's "Hallowfair" and "Leith Races", the greater intellectual resources available to Burns at once become apparent.

In "The Farmer's Ingle" Fergusson has little to offer in competition.

He is patronizing about superstition, but limits its effects to children and the very old. (Again, contrast Burns in "Hallowe'en", a poem which it is not at present fashionable to admire). The church and the minister make their only appearance in terms of the stock comedy of the cutty stool. The Devil is nowhere mentioned. Fergusson's knowledge here, and indeed in all his poems, seems to lack inwardness; he is unreligious rather than irreligious in a way the more surprising when one recollects that he died in the Edinburgh Bedlam, a victim, if we accept Mr McDiarmid's findings[15], of religious mania and syphilis.

The Caledonian Antisyzygy is very much a creation of the Enlightenment, and Fergusson may be regarded as the most eminent victim of the disease. With one part of his mind he strove to be detached, sceptical, even cynical – the pure observer who at the same time was a Tory and *laudator temporis acti*, always provided that certain aspects of the past might be left entirely out of the reckoning. In this mood he was totally indifferent to the religion of his immediate ancestors and most of his contemporaries. It is this mood which finds expression in the poems under discussion. Alexander Peterkin, in his biography of the poet, has this passage derived from an unnamed informant[16]:—

> "He also introduced the Christian Religion, and conversed with much earnestness on some of its fundamental doctrines. Upon a particular occasion, which he specified, he said a Mr Ferrier, at or near St Andrews, had alarmed and rather displeased him, by maintaining what are usually denominated the orthodox tenets of our Scotch creeds: and Fergusson appeared to differ, in a very considerable degree, from the commonly received notion on these subjects. He did not seem to be satisfied of the necessity of the fall of man, and of a mediatorial sacrifice for human iniquity; and he questioned, with considerable boldness, the consistency of such doctrines, with the attributes of divine wisdom and goodness. At the same time, however, he confessed the imperfect nature of human intellect, and the unfathomable depth of all such enquiries."

Several points here require expansion. Fergusson obviously had moved at least on the direction of Hume and Voltaire. His emphasis on divine wisdom and goodness is in the tradition of the moderate *philosophes*. It seems that by choice he would have taken an optimistic and generally secular and humanistic view of human life and its prospects.

Characteristically, he was at the same time nervous of giving full adherence to the philosophic views which he found congenial.

The doctrines which displeased and alarmed him, especially "the *necessity"* (my italics) "of the fall of man and of a mediatorial sacrifice", were the orthodox Calvinistic doctrines of pre-destination, as expressed by Thomas Boston, and satirized in later literary terms by *The Private Memoirs and Confessions of a Justified Sinner* and by "Holy Willie's Prayer"[17]:—

> O Thou that in the Heavens does dwell,
> Wha, as it pleases best Thysel,
> Sends ane to Heaven an' ten to Hell
> A' for Thy glory,
> And no for onie guid or ill
> They've done before Thee!
>
> (1–6)

As a poet, Fergusson was a rationalist, who combined his rationalism with a strong attachment to the past, and, partly as a consequence, conveyed it, not by direct statement, but by silences and implications. His views may have been more extreme than those of Burns, but nothing in his poetry corresponds to the ecclesiastical satires already mentioned, to "The Twa Herds" or to "The Kirk's Alarm". He never spoke out – perhaps, even probably, as the result of an inner conflict like that which destroyed Cowper and crippled Gray. In the part of his mind which held firmly to the past, he was still haunted by the terrors of orthodox Calvinism.

This is not to deny that much of his poetry is satiric. The truth is almost the reverse. But the satire is not religious. To a great extent, as in "Hallowfair", and "Leith Races", it is descriptive and confined to the odd, the old-fashioned, the extravagant – more generally, to whatever unpleasantly affects the five external senses. Fergusson's poetry was much affected by his acute physical and nervous sensitivity, as may be seen from "Auld Reekie", or the grizzly detail of his English masterpiece, "The Sow of Feeling", and it is as a consequence that he lays so much emphasis on the cleanliness of the idealized farm in "The Farmer's Ingle". In such poems, his physical perceptions rather than his speculative intellect are engaged. The speculative intellect, however, could operate by way of physical perceptions in one sphere – the economic – and some of Fergusson's most satisfying poetry deals with the new Economic Man, whose standards had begun to dominate Edinburgh society In "The Ghaists", for instance, he finds types of the more liberal older order in George Heriot (1563–1624) and George Watson (died 1723), two Edinburgh burgesses who had left their fortunes to found schools for the poor children of decayed Edinburgh burgesses.

This generosity had its appropriate physical symbol in the schoolbuildings, which faced each other beside Greyfriars' Kirkyaird where so many distinguished Edinburgh citizens were buried, and where the ghosts of the two pious founders might conveniently foregather. The new order is symbolised by the proposed Mortmain Bill (1773), which was eventually withdrawn, but which in effect was to transfer the control of hereditary charities from the trustees to the London government, and which, Fergusson thought, would thus bring the benefactions of Heriot and Watson to an abrupt and sordid end. The theme is distantly related to that of "The Farmer's Ingle", but the treatment is more direct and powerful[18]:—

> Black be the day that e'er to England's ground
> Scotland was eikit by the Union's bond;
> For mony a menzie of destructive ills
> The country now maun brook frae *mortmain bills*,
> That void our test'ments, and can freely gie
> Sic will and scoup to the ordain'd trustee,
> That he may tir our stateliest riggins bare,
> Nor acres, houses, woods nor fishins spare,
> Till he can lend the stoitering state a lift
> Wi' gowd in gowpins as a grassum gift;
> In lieu o' whilk, we maun be wal content
> To tyne the capital at three *per cent.*
> A doughty sum indeed, whan now-a-days
> They raise provisions, as the stents they raise,
> Yoke hard the poor, and lat the rich chiels be,
> Pamper'd at ease by ither's industry.
>   Hale interest for my fund can scantly now
> Cleed a' my callant's backs, and stap their mou'.
> How maun their weyms wi' sairest hunger slack,
> Their duds in targets flaff upo' their back,
> Whan they are doom'd to keep a lasting Lent,
> Starving for England's weel at *three per cent.*
>   (57–78)

Fergusson's attitude here is almost the reverse of Thomson's in *The Seasons*. For Thomson, England represented the generous present and abundant future, Scotland the limited, unfortunate and poverty-stricken past. Fergusson's hostility to the Union is directed, not so much at England, as at the capitalism with its narrow emphasis on the cash-nexus, of which he takes England to be the type, and which he feared with justification that all too many of his countrymen were ready to accept:—

There's einow on the earth a set o' men,
Wha, if they get their private pouches lin'd
Gie na a winnelstrae for a' mankind;
They'll sell their country, flae their conscience bare,
To gar the weigh-bank turn a single hair,
The government need only bait the line
Wi' the prevailing flee, the gowden coin,
Then our executors, and wise trustees,
Will sell them fishes in forbidden seas,
Upo' their dwining country girn in sport,
Laugh in their sleeve, and get a place at court.

                                            (104–114)

For Fergusson however an attachment to the older economic order, and an avoidance, no matter what his own opinions might be, of religious comment in his poetry, offered no prophylactic against the Calvinist nightmare. The story of the incident which put him fully on the road to insanity shows how feeble the barriers were. I quote Gleig's version[19]:—

> " 'In the room adjoining to that in which he slept was a starling, which being seized one night by a cat that had found its way down the chimney, awaked Mr Fergusson by the most alarming screams. Having learned the cause of his alarm, he began seriously to reflect how often he, an immortal and accountable being, had in the hour of intemperance set death at defiance, though it was thus terrible in reality to an unaccountable and sinless creature.' " Such thoughts " 'aided by the solemnity of midnight, wrought his mind up to a pitch of remorse that almost bordered on frantic despair.' " As a consequence, he burned every scrap of his writings, saying " 'I am satisfied – I feel some consolation in never having written anything against religion.' "

Within a short time, he was overtaken by the religious delusions which eventually brought him to the madhouse. "He was one day met below the North Bridge by a gentleman with whom he had formerly been very intimately connected; and as he seemed to pass on quite regardless of every surrounding object, his friend accosted him, and demanded of him whither he was going. He replied that he had just discovered one of the reprobates who crucified our Saviour, and that in order to have him disposed of according to law, he was making all possible haste to lodge the information with Lord Kames."

Fergusson died in Bedlam a few months later, six weeks after his twenty fourth birthday.

One must exercise extreme caution in any attempt to analyse the mental processes of someone dead for two hundred years. It seems fairly clear, nevertheless, that in Fergusson poetry and religion stood in acute opposition to each other, that during his most creative period, poetry kept the upper hand, but that latterly religion made a destructive return in the form of obsession. Fergusson's life is a briefer, more lurid version of the English poet Cowper's – more lurid, because in his poetry, as in his life, Fergusson ranged over a field of experience much wider than was ever open to Cowper. Between Cowper's poetry and his religion there is almost no gap of the kind one discovers in Fergusson; religious despair is present in "The Castaway", but absent to an ultimately surprising extent from "Braid Claith" or "Auld Reikie". Only for a few lines in the latter poem does any hint of hidden fear come to the surface[20]:—

> In Morning, whan ane keeks about,
> Fu' blyth and free frae Ail, nae doubt
> He lippens not to be misled
> Among the Regions of the dead:
> But straight a painted Corp he sees,
> Lang streekit 'neath its Canopies,
> Soon, soon will this his Mirth controul,
> And send Damnation to his Soul:
> Or when the Dead-deal (awful Shape!)
> Makes frighted Mankind girn and gape,
> Reflection then his Reason sours,
> For the niest Dead-deal may be ours.
> Whan Sybyl led the Trojan down
> To haggard PLUTO'S dreary town,
> Shapes war nor thae, I freely ween
> Cou'd never meet the Soldier's Ein.
>
> (179–194)

Within a few lines, however, he was returned to the physical sensations with which the poem is primarily concerned:—

> The Birks sae green, and sweet Brier-thorn,
> Wi' sprangit Flow'rs that scent the Gale,
> Ca' far awa' the Morning Smell,
> Wi' which our ladies Flow'r-pat's fill'd
>
> (204–207)

The very acuteness of his physical sensibilities, as clearly demonstrated in these lines as in the story of the cat and the starling, contributed to the strength of his final obsession. In the Scots poetry, for the most part, the two are held separate, at least partly because Fergusson had undergone the liberating effect, however temporary it proved, of Enlightenment scepticism, resulting from theories of divine benevolence and the natural man. Of these ideas, the clearest and simplest expression is to be found in the pastoral "Night", which was published in Ruddiman's *Weekly Magazine* in February, 1771, before he had made his name as a poet in Scots[21]:—

AMYNTAS
What mighty power conducts the stars on high!
Who bids these comets thro' our system fly!
Who wafts the light'ning to the icy pole!
And thro' our regions bids the thunders roll!

FLORELLUS
But say, what mightier power from nought could raise
The earth, the sun, and all that fiery maze
Of distant stars that gild the azure sky,
And thro' the void in settled orbits fly?

AMYNTAS
That righteous Power, before whose heavenly eye
The stars are nothing, and the planets die;
Whose breath divine supports our mortal frame,
Who made the lion wild, and lambkin tame.

FLORELLUS
At his command the bounteous spring returns;
Hot summer, raging o'er the Atlantic burns;
The yellow autumn crowns our sultry toil,
And winter's snows prepare the cumb'rous soil.

AMYNTAS
By him the morning darts her purple ray;
To him the birds their early homage pay;
With vocal harmony the meadows ring,
While swains in concert heav'nly praises sing.

FLORELLUS
Swayed by his word the nutrient dews descend,
And growing pastures to the moisture bend;

The vernal blossoms sip his falling showers;
The meads are garnish'd with his opening flow'rs.

AMYNTAS

For *man*, the object of his chiefest care,
Fowls he hath form'd to wing the ambient air,
For him the *steer* his lusty neck doth bend;
Fishes for him their scaly fins extend.

FLORELLUS

Wide o'er the orient sky the moon appears,
A foe to darkness and his idle fears;
Around her orb the stars in clusters shine
And distant planets tend her silver shrine.

$$(21–52)$$

The poem has no philosophic or theological consistency. Calvinism shows in one couplet, the most energetic in the poem:—

That righteous Power, before whose heavenly eye
The stars are nothing, and the planets die.

The subject of the poem however is theology, as formulated by natural man. The theology itself combines several elements. The references to comets, the void, and settled orbits are Newtonian. The principle of plenitude, as an explanation and justification of the existence of evil, underlies the reference to the lion and the lambkin; Isaiah's paradox of reconciliation has been forgotten or suppressed. The humanistic idea that as the result of divine benevolence the universe exists primarily for man's benefit, appears in the five final stanzas quoted. It was by such devious routes as this that Fergusson's own natural man was released to write poetry, not in English, but in Scots.

In Scotland, as was seen by the Catholic priest Dr Alexander Geddes (1737–1802) in his "Epistle to the President, Vice-Presidents, and Members of the Scottish Society of Antiquaries, On being chosen a Correspondent Member" (1792), the language of the natural man was Scots[22]:—

Let bragart England in disdain
Ha'd ilka lingo, but her a'in:
Her a'in, we wat, say what she can,
Is like her true-born Englishman,
A vile promiscuous mungrel seed
Of Danish, Dutch, an' Norman breed,

An' prostituted, since, to a'
The jargons on this earthly ba'!
Bedek't, 'tis true, an' made fu' smart
Wi' mekil learning, pains an' art;
An taught to baik, an' benge, an' bou
As dogs an' dancin'-masters do:
Wi' fardit cheeks an' pouder't hair,
An' brazen confidential stare –
While ours, a blate an' bashfu' maid
Conceals her blushes wi' her plaid;
And is unwillan' to display
Her beuties in the face o' day.
    Bot strip them baith – an' see wha's shape
Has least the semblance of an ape?
Wha's lims are straightest? Wha can sheu
The whiter skin, an' fairer heu;
An' whilk, in short, is the mair fit
To gender genuine manly wit?
I'll pledge my pen, you'll judgment pass
In favor of the Scottis lass

                              (115–131)

It is important to emphasize the extent to which Geddes is writing, not merely from prejudice, but, in a way appropriate to a Correspondent Member of the Society of Antiquaries, from knowledge of the linguistic and lexicographical studies of the later seventeenth and eighteenth centuries, which themselves formed part of the Enlightenment. The poem was printed in a learned article entitled "Three Scottish Poems with a previous Dissertation on the Scoto-Saxon Dialect", and in a footnote to the passage quoted Geddes refers the reader to the *Linguarum Veterum Septentrionalium Thesaurus grammatico-criticus et archaeologicus* (1703–1705) of the celebrated George Hickes (1642–1715).

For Fergusson, unfortunately, it was all too easy to identify the natural man of the *philosophes* with the Old Man, the Old Adam of Pauline and Calvinist theology: this, I suggest, explains how for him religion and poetry came to be destructively opposed[23]:—

O had ye seen, as I hae seen him,
Whan nae *Blue Devils* did pervene him
An' heard the *pipe* the Lord had gi'en him
    In *Scottish air*
Ye'd ablins for an angel ta'n him,
    He sang sae rare

> But whan by these d — — — — d fiends attacket,
> His fine-spun saul they hav'd an' hacket,
> Your very heart-strings wad hae cracket
>   To've seen him than;
> He was just like a headless tacket,
>   In shape o' man,
>
> (43–54)

This, at the same time, is still to leave Enlightenment ideas as prime instruments in the production of Fergusson's best poetry. The movement towards the writing of these poems is almost an exact antithesis of that which in the sixteenth and seventeenth centuries came close to extinguishing poetry written in Scots. I have suggested elsewhere[24] that the earlier development is most clearly visible in the work of the musician and poet, Alexander Scott (c. 1515–1584), who began as an author of sensual and cynical love songs, and of comic poems in the tradition of "Christ's Kirk on the Green", but who ended, after the Reformation, as a satiric and censorial moralist, who may have entirely given over literary work in the last fifteen to twenty years of his life. The Reformation, the establishment of Presbyterianism, and the religious wars of the seventeenth century are, it seems to me, much more important than the Union of the Crowns as factors to explain the relative lack of Scots poetry in the century and a half which followed the death of Alexander Scott. Scots as a literary language lost prestige among Presbyterians, not so much because the court language, as because the church language, had become English, and because composition in Scots had become identified with conservative religious views and the licentious life of the old order. The Enlightenment gave Scots poetry the opportunity to reassert itself. Conservatism meant attachment to the past, but when the past society could be regarded as simpler and more egalitarian than the present, conservatism was soon combined with idealization of the ancestral natural man and his language. (A similar development is to be observed in Macpherson). For Fergusson as for Burns, free-living as well as free-thinking belonged to the natural man – the licentiousness of the older literature, and of the sub-culture in which it had survived and developed, answered a philosophic as well as a physical need.

Free-loving and free-thinking alike were opposed to the Presbyterian establishment, and conservatism often entailed an attachment to papistical or episcopalian views, which to much of the Church were as anti-clerical as free-thinking itself. To an astonishing extent, the Scottish Enlightenment was precisely adapted to release these literary forces which had been suppressed or dormant since the Reformation. Burns most completely mastered every aspect of the new situation. The tension between new and old rapidly became too much for Fergusson.

NOTES

1. J. H. Millar, *A Literary History of Scotland* (London, 1903), 370.
2. M. P. McDiarmid, *The Poems of Robert Fergusson* (S.T.S., 2 vols., Edinburgh and London, 1954, 1956), I.11.
3. Craig, *op. cit.*, 15.
4. Margaret Wattie (ed.), *The Scottish Works of Alexander Ross, M. A., Schoolmaster at Lochlee* (S.T.S., Edinburgh and London, 1938), 6.
5. Wattie, *op. cit.*, 81–82.
6. *Op. cit.*, xlii–xliii.
7. "Eighteenth-Century Vernacular Poetry" in J. Kinsley (ed.), *Scottish Poetry. A Critical Survey* (London, 1955), 180.
8. Ibid.
9. Chapter VII.
10. McDiarmid, *op. cit.*, II.137.
11. "The Taill of the Wolf and the Lamb", Elliott, *op. cit*, 82–83.
12. Quoted in H. Hamilton, *An Economic History of Scotland in the Eighteenth Century* (Oxford, 1963), 73.
13. Kinsley, *Burns*, I.145–152.
14. Kinsley, *Burns*, I.128–137.
15. McDiarmid, *op. cit.*, I.69–79.
16. McDiarmid, *op. cit.*, I.71–72.
17. Kinsley, *Burns*, I.74–78.
18. McDiarmid, *op. cit.*, II.143.
19. McDiarmid, *op. cit.*, I. 72–73.
20. McDiarmid, *op. cit.*, II.114–115.
21. McDiarmid, *op. cit.*, II.14–16.
22. *Transactions of the Society of the Antiquaries of Scotland* 1 (Edinburgh, 1792), 400–468.
23. McDiarmid, *op. cit.*, 108–109. The quotation is from the anonymous "Epistle to Robert Burns, The Ayrshire Poet" which appeared in *The Edinburgh Evening Courant*, 12 December, 1786.
24. MacQueen *Ballattis of Luve* (Edinburgh, 1970), xi–xvii.

CHAPTER VII

SYNTHESIS AND
TRANSCENDENCE: Robert Burns

Where Fergusson had been silent, Burns was explicit. His attack on the Auld Lichts paralleled, but was fiercer and wider-ranging than that of Ramsay and Clerk on the Covenanters. In ironic verve he rivals even Voltaire[1]:—

> Hypocrisy, in mercy spare it!
> That *holy robe*, O dinna tear it!
> Spare't for their sakes wha aften wear it,
>   The lads in *black*;
> But your curst wit, when it comes near it,
>   Rives't off their back.
>
> Think, wicked Sinner, wha ye're skaithing:
> It's just the *Blue-gown* badge an' claithing,
> O' Saunts; tak that, ye lea'e them naething,
>   To ken them by,
> Frae only unregenerate Heathen,
>   Like you or I.
>   (13–24)

He recognized and rejected the all too frequent association of strict Calvinism with the more grasping form of capitalistic ethics, represented by Holy Willie's prayer for "grace and gear"[2]:—

> Were this the *charter* of our state,
> 'On pain o' *hell* be rich an' great,'
> *Damnation* then would be our fate,
>   Beyond remead;
> But, thanks to Heav'n, that's no the gate
>   We learn our *creed*.
>   (79–84)

(The emphasis in this last line should fall on "we" and "our". Burns implies that the creed of others differs.) His knowledge of the new physics and astronomy, with their undertones of materialism, or at least deism, while less precise than that of Thomson or Fergusson, was used to effective satiric purpose[3]:—

> In days when mankind were but callans,
> At *Grammar, Logic*, an' sic talents,
> They took nae pains their speech to balance,
>   Or rules to gie,
> But spak their thoughts in plain, braid lallans,
>   Like you or me.
>
> In thae auld times, they thought the *Moon*,
> Just like a sark, or pair o' shoon,
> Woor by degrees, till her last roon
>   Gaed past their viewin,
> An' shortly after she was done
>   They gat a new ane.
>
> This past for certain, undisputed;
> It ne'er cam i' their heads to doubt it,
> Till chiels gat up an' wad confute it,
>   An' ca'd it wrang;
> An' muckle din there was about it,
>   Baith loud an' lang.
>
>   (115–132)

With a twist very characteristic of· Burns, it is the Auld Lichts who decide to make use of the experimental method and the latest advances in technology to confute their heretical brethren, who accept the Newtonian universe:—

> But shortly they will cowe the louns!
> Some *auld-light herds* in neebor towns
> Are mind't, in things they ca' *balloons*.
>   To tak a flight,
> An' stay ae month amang the *Moons*
>   An see them right.
>
> Guid observation they will gie them;
> An' when the *auld Moon's* gaun to lea'e them,
> The hindmost *shaird*, they'll fetch it wi' them,
>   Just i' their pouch,

> An' when the *new-light* billies see them,
>   I think they'll crouch!
>   (169–180)

Burns certainly possessed something of the spirit of *le conte philosophique* and used it for purposes not unlike those of his French contemporaries.

It is more, however, by what he implies than by what he says that Burns shows himself a man of the Enlightenment. Generally he stops short of the undisguised scepticism of Hume or Smollett, and as a consequence makes it easier to see the Kirk satires as merely local phenomena, to find in them that limitation to "Scotch drink, Scotch manners, Scotch religion" which Matthew Arnold[4] from the safe distance of Dover Beach found so distressing. It is certainly true that for Burns the declared target always remained the Auld Lichts, and that in themselves the Auld Lichts were local and limited. Holy Willie, on the other hand, based though he is on a single Auld Licht elder, is a figure of greater universality than Dryden's Zimri or MacFlecknoe; the Unco Guid appear in communities far separated from rural Ayrshire; *mutatis mutandis* they are as characteristic of twentieth century London or Peking as of eighteenth century Galston. On the evidence simply of what he has written, it is as reasonable to identify Burns with the New Lichts as Voltaire with the Quakers or Freemasons.

ii

Literary form is as important for Burns as for any other major poet, but in the past this aspect of his work has not often received the attention it deserves. *Tam o' Shanter*, for instance, is probably the best-known of his longer poems, with an opening as familiar as anything he ever wrote[5]:—

> When chapman billies leave the street,
> And drouthy neebors, neebors meet,
> As market-days are wearing late,
> An' folk begin to tak the gate;
> While we sit bousing at the nappy,
> And getting fou and unco happy,
> We think na on the lang Scots miles,
> The mosses, waters, slaps and styles,
> That lie between us and our hame,
> Whare sits our sulky, sullen dame,
> Gathering her brows like gathering storm,
> Nursing her wrath to keep it warm.
>   (1–12)

For most people, this familiarity has hidden how unusual a poem *Tam o'*
Shanter in fact is, unusual in relation not only to Burns's work as a whole,
but even to the general course of later Scottish literature. Save in the
ballads, the short story in verse scarcely figures there at all. In Burns
himself or in Fergusson there is nothing comparable; very little in
Ramsay, and before him we have to go back to Lindsay's *Squyer Meldrum*
(*c.* 1550), which in some ways does bear a close resemblance to *Tam o'*
Shanter. Burns himself set the poem apart by his sub-title, "A Tale", still
more by his prefatory quotation, "Of Brownyis and of Bogillis full is
this buke". Such prefatory verses are not uncommon. Sometimes Burns
uses them to indicate the tone and subject-matter of the following poem,
the tradition in which it is written, as for instance in *The Cotter's Saturday*
Night[6], to which he prefixed lines from Gray's *Elegy*:—

> Let not Ambition mock their useful toil,
> Their homely joys, and destiny obscure;
> Nor Grandeur hear, with a disdainful smile,
> The short and simple annals of the poor.

Alternatively, the quotation may serve as a text, on which the succeed-
ing poem is a satirical variation, as in the *Address to the Deil*[7], to which
Burns prefixed the lines from *Paradise Lost* I, in which Beelzebub
addresses Satan:—

> O Prince! O Chief of many thronèd powers!
> That led th'embattled seraphim to war.

Generally it may be said that Burns's quotations are from eighteenth
century English or Scots poetry, sometimes from Milton or Shakespeare,
or adapted versions of biblical texts. As opposed to this, the prefatory
verse to *Tam o' Shanter* is taken from the Prologue to the translation of
the sixth book of the *Aeneid* by Gavin Douglas, bishop of Dunkeld. This
was completed in 1513. The subject of the sixth book is the descent of
Aeneas to the underworld, and in his Prologue Douglas emphasizes that
the book is something more than a record of superstitious fantasies[8]:—

> Quhat? Wenis fulis this sext buke bene bot japis,
> All full of leis or ald idolatreis?
> O hald your pece, ye verray goddis apis!
> Reid, reid agane, this volume, mair than tuise;
> Consider quhat hid sentence tharin lyis.
>
>   (9–13)

Douglas, in fact, is *not* content to say of the sixth book that it is full of
brownies and bogles, and the phrase "hid sentence" ("concealed

meaning") has more than a passing relevance to Burn's own poem.
    A third point may be noted. Some time before he wrote the poem in
1790, Burns produced a prose version of the narrative in a letter (No.
401⁹) to his friend, the antiquary Captain Francis Grose. The version is
interesting in itself, as also because the story is only one of three, and
details from the other two have found a place in the poem – a minor but
striking illustration of the esemplastic vitality of Burns's imagination.
The stylistic contrast of prose and verse is notable. (I quote only the first
two stories):—
    "Among the many Witch Stories I have heard relating to
Aloway Kirk, I distinctly remember only two or three.
    Upon a stormy night, amid whirling squalls of wind and
bitter blasts of hail, in short, on such a night as the devil would
chuse to take the air in, a farmer or a farmer's servant was
plodding and plashing homeward with his plough-irons on his
shoulder, having been getting some repairs on them at a
neighbouring smithy. His way lay by the Kirk of Aloway, and
being rather on the anxious look-out in approaching a place so
well known to be a favourite haunt of the devil and the devil's
friends and emissaries, he was struck aghast by discovering,
through the horrors of the storm and stormy night, a light,
which, on his nearer approach, plainly shewed itself to proceed
from the haunted edifice. Whether he had been fortified from
above on his devout supplication, as is customary with people
when they suspect the immediate presence of Satan; or
whether, according to another custom, he had got
courageously drunk at the smithy, I will not pretend to
determine; but so it was that he ventured to go up to, nay into
the very Kirk. – As good luck would have it, his temerity came
off unpunished. The members of the infernal junto were all out
on some midnight business or other, and he saw nothing but a
kind of kettle or caldron, depending from the roof, over the
fire, simmering some heads of unchristened children, limbs of
executed malefactors &c. for the business of the night. It was, in
for a penny, in for a pound, with the honest ploughman; so
without ceremony he unhooked the caldron from off the fire,
and pouring out the damnable ingredients, inverted it on his
head, and carried it fairly home, where it remained long in the
family a living evidence of the truth of the story.
    Another story, which I can prove to be equally authentic,
was as follows.
    On a market in the town of Ayr, a farmer from Carrick, and

consequently whose way lay by the very gate of Aloway kirk-
yard, in order to cross the river Doon at the old bridge, which
is about two or three hundred yards further on than the said
gate, had been detained by his business till by the time he
reached Aloway it was the wizard hour, between night and
morning.

Though he was terrified with a blaze streaming from the
kirk, yet as it is a well known fact, that to turn back on these
occasions is running by far the greatest risk of mischief, he
prudently advanced on his road. When he had reached the
gate of the kirk-yard, he was surprised and entertained,
through the ribs and arches of an old gothic window which
still faces the highway, to see a dance of witches merrily
footing it round their old sooty blackguard master, who was
keeping them all alive with the power of his bagpipe. The
farmer stopping his horse to observe them a little, could plainly
descry the faces of many old women of his acquaintance and
neighbourhood. How the gentleman was dressed, tradition
does not say; but the ladies were all in their smocks; and one of
them happening unluckily to have a smock which was
considerably too short to answer all the purpose of that piece
of dress, our farmer was so tickled that he involuntarily burst
out, with a loud laugh, 'Weel luppen, Maggy wi' the short
sark!' and recollecting himself, instantly spurred his horse to
the top of his speed. I need not mention the universally known
fact, that no diabolical power can pursue you beyond the
middle of a running stream. Lucky it was for the poor farmer
that the river Doon was so near, for notwithstanding the speed
of his horse, which was a good one, against he reached the
middle of the arch of the bridge, and consequently the middle
of the stream, the pursuing, vengeful hags were so close at his
heels, that one of them actually sprung to seize him: but it was
too late; nothing was on her side of the stream but the horse's
tail, which immediately gave way to her infernal grip, as if
blasted by a stroke of lightning; but the farmer was beyond her
reach. – However, the unsightly, tailless condition of the
vigorous steed was to the last hours of the noble creature's life,
an awful warning to the Carrick farmers, not to stay too late in
Ayr markets.–"

Tam o' Shanter was probably written in late 1790. The letter to Captain
Grose shows that the matter of the poem was already occupying his mind

in the earlier part of the year. Still earlier – in April 1788, to be more exact – Burns, as is indicated by letters (238 and 241) to Mrs Dunlop, had read Dryden's translation of Virgil, and in particular the *Georgics* and the *Aeneid*. His mind at the time was unusually occupied with classical and heroic poetry – Homer and Tasso as well as Virgil[10]:—

"Dryden's Virgil has delighted me. – I do not know whether the Critics will agree with me, but the Georgics are to me by far the best of Virgil. – It is indeed a species of writing entirely new to me; and has filled my head with a thousand fancies of emulation: but, alas! when I read the Georgics, and then survey my own powers, 'tis like the idea of a Shetland Pony, drawn up by the side of a thorough-bred Hunter, to start for the Plate –
I own I am disappointed in the Aeneid. – Faultless correctness may please, and does highly please, the letter'd Critic; but to that awful character I have not the most distant pretensions. – I don't know whether I do not hazard my pretensions to be a Critic of any kind, when I say that I think Virgil, in many instances, a *servile* Copier of Homer. – If I had the Odyssey by me, I could parallel many passages where Virgil has evidently copied *but by no means improved* Homer. Nor can I think there is anything of this owing to the translators; for, from everything I have seen of Dryden, I think him, in genius and fluency of language, Pope's master. I have not perused Tasso enough, to form an opinion: in some future letter, you shall have my ideas of him; tho' I am conscious my criticisms must be very inaccurate and imperfect, as *there* I have ever felt and lamented my want of learning most."

This last may seem to lead us rather far from *Tam o' Shanter*, although even in such a context the prefatory quotation from Gavin Douglas suggests some relationship to Burns's reading in Virgil. Douglas in the sixteenth century had successfully translated Virgil's heroic poem into Scots, and in the eighteenth century his translation was regarded as the chief ornament of early Scottish literature. The Scots themselves had produced two other epics, the *Bruce* of John Barbour and the *Wallace* of Hary, the second of which was certainly known to Burns; it "poured a Scottish prejudice in my veins which will boil along there till the flood-gates of life shut in eternal rest."[11] As is evidenced, for instance, by Wilkie, Macpherson and, in a different context, Donnchadh Bán, the heroic considered as the most exalted form of the natural in man, was a matter of critical and philosophical, as well as emotional, concern to eighteenth-century Scots. The point is relevant to Burns: in *Tam o' Shanter*, I suggest, he was engaged in an enterprise which had some

similarity to those of Douglas, Barbour and Hary. In particular, like
Aeneas in Virgil's Book VI, Tam o' Shanter pays a visit to the
Otherworld. The poem too is heroic at least to the extent that the adjec-
tive is once applied to Tam:—

> Coffins stood round, like open presses,
> That show'd the dead in their last dresses;
> And by some devilish cantraip slight
> Each in its cauld land held a light. –
> By which heroic *Tam* was able
> To note upon the haly table,
> A murderer's banes in gibbet airns – – –
> (125–131)

and so on, through the long ghastly catalogue which emerged from the
description in letter 401 of the contents of the cauldron. "Heroic" as an
attributive adjective is the more notable in that it is one of only two such
applied to Tam in the entire poem. The other is "honest", and it is
applied to Tam when he makes his first entrance:—

> This truth fand honest *Tam o' Shanter*,
> As he frae Ayr ae night did canter,
> (Auld Ayr, wham ne'er a town surpasses,
> For honest men and bonny lasses.)
> (13–16)

(The repetition of the adjective links Tam to the prosaic burgess world of
the market town – the world of Galt's *The Provost*.)

For Burns the adjective "honest" had a particular significance which,
one would imagine, is as far removed from "heroic" as is well possible
for it to be. I quote for instance, from *The Cotter's Saturday Night*:—

> From Scenes like these, old Scotia's grandeur springs,
> That makes her lov'd at home, rever'd abroad:
> Princes and lords are but the breath of kings,
> 'An honest man's the noblest work of God.'
> (163–166)

The last line is misquoted from Pope's *Essay on Man* IV, 248, but in such a
context as to make it clear that for Burns the word "honest" properly
applied to classes almost the antithesis of potentially heroic princes and
lords. "Is there, for honest poverty?" he begins another familiar poem[12],
which again sneers at princes and lords.

In *Tam o' Shanter* kings once appear in a single brief contrast with

Tam, and in a passage almost halfway between the two adjectives I have mentioned — a passage in which two further adjectives are applied to him, this time, however, predicatively. The scene is the Ayr inn:—

> Care, mad to see a man sae happy,
> E'en drown'd himsel amang the nappy:
> As bees flee hame wi' lades o' treasure.
> The minutes wing'd their way wi' pleasure:
> Kings may be blest, but *Tam* was glorious,
> O'er a' the ills o' life victorious.
>
> (53–58)

The transition, that is to say, is not directly from "honest" to "heroic", but by way of "glorious" and "victorious". The stages of the transition are thus rendered more credible, particularly when one remembers the objective correlative in terms of which they are expressed — drink. An honest man spends an evening at the inn, and is gradually transformed by glory and victory to a hero.

"A small man is not in himself a ridiculous object: he becomes ridiculous when he is dressed up in a suit of armour designed for a hero." So Mr Ian Jack[13] in a discussion of Dryden's mock-heroic *Mac Flecknoe*. The point towards which the discussion has been rather laboriously tending is that, like *Mac Flecknoe, Absalom and Achitophel, The Rape of the Lock* and *The Dunciad, Tam o' Shanter* is essentially a mock-heroic poem in the classical tradition of the Enlightenment, with the additional complication that it is a mock-heroic constructed in terms, not of London aristocratic or literary society, but of the life of the Scots peasantry. The constituent elements are Virgil, as interpreted on the one hand by Dryden, on the other by Douglas; the Augustan mock-heroic tradition with its French and Latin roots; ideas on natural man and the heroic, current in eighteenth-century Scotland, and the folk-tales recorded by Burns in his letter to Captain Grose. In the way discussed in the fifth chapter of this book, the classical form expresses the ironic secularism which characterizes the treatment in the poem of Satan and the witches.

Many of the complexities of *Tam o' Shanter* find their essential pattern once this central fact has been realized. Like the diction of *The Rape of the Lock*, and to some extent of mock-heroic generally, that of *Tam o' Shanter* (to quote J. S. Cunningham[14]) "runs with a self-delighting dexterity, through a wide range of attitudes, commanding a startling variety of tones". Much good recent criticism, particularly that of Professor Daiches[15] and Mr Crawford[16], has been directed to this feature. All I wish to add is the convenience of regarding the differences of attitude and tone in terms not so much of "voices" as of levels of diction and style. Burns's diction varies from what might be termed high, through middle, to low; the high represented for instance, by a transitional passage, the language of which is often described as English:—

> But pleasures are like poppies spread,
> You seize the flower, its bloom is shed;
> Or like the snow falls in the river,
> A moment white – then melts for ever;
> Or like the borealis race,
> That flit ere you can point their place;
> Or like the rainbow's lovely form
> Evanishing amid the storm
>
> (59–66)

The middle is represented by the lines into which the passage modulates:—

> Na man can tether time or tide;
> The hour approaches *Tam* maun ride
>
> (67–68)

the low by such a passage as:—

> She tauld thee weel thou was a skellum,
> A blethering, blustering, drunken blellum;
> That frae November till October,
> Ae market-day thou was nae sober;
> That ilka melder, wi' the miller,
> Thou sat as lang as thou had siller;
> That every naig was ca'd a shoe on,
> The smith and thee gat roaring fou on.
>
> (19–26)

But distinct from his range of diction, Burns also has a high, middle and low range of style, which in any particular passage need not precisely correspond to the level of diction. Indeeed, a counterpoint of stylistic level and level of diction is one of the main artistic devices in the poem. Formal narrative transitions, for instance, are a characteristic stylistic feature of English heroic and mock-heroic verse – that is to say of high style or mock-high style. Professor Tillotson has quoted[17] from *The Rape of the Lock* the transition from Belinda's success at cards to her fall at the coffee-table:—

> O thoughtless mortals! ever blind to fate,
> Too soon dejected, and too soon elate.
> Sudden these honours shall be snatch'd away,
> And curs'd for ever this victorious day.
>
> (iii.101–104)

In the first two passages quoted to illustrate the different levels of diction, Burns makes a transition in this very fashion. (The assumed voice is that of the poet, inspired by the Muse with superhuman insight.) Compare too, and note the lower stylistic level:—

> Ah, gentle dames! it gars me greet,
> To think how mony counsels sweet,
> How mony lengthen'd sage advices,
> The husband frae the wife despises!
>
> (33–36)

Again, in mock-heroic, the inspired narrator may intervene directly:—

> Ah! cease rash Youth! desist ere 'tis too late,
> Fear the just Gods, and think of Scylla's Fate!
>
> (iii.121–122)

Compare:—

> Now, *Tam*, O *Tam*! had thae been queans,
> A' plump and strapping in their teens –
>
> (151–152)

or the immortal:—

> Ah, *Tam*! Ah, *Tam*! thou'll get thy fairin!
> In hell they'll roast thee like a herrin!
>
> (201–202)

Burns is deliberately exploiting the combination of low diction with epic narrative progression.

In accordance with traditional practice, Dryden began *Mac Flecknoe* with a grave *sententia*[18]:—

> All humane things are subject to decay,
> And, when Fate summons, Monarchs must obey.
>
> (1–2)

This is distinguished from the genuine heroic only by the beginning of the *prosecutio* which follows, "This *Fleckno* found".

The opening of *Tam o' Shanter* is similar, but more elaborate. Burns too begins with a *sententia* followed by the *prosecutio*, in which Tam is introduced and dubbed as "honest":—

> This truth fand honest *Tam o' Shanter*,
> As he frae Ayr ae night did canter,
>
> (13–14)

The *sententia* however is less abstract, less elevated, and expressed in the first person:—

> While we sit bousing at the nappy,
> And getting fou and unco happy,
> We think na on the lang Scots miles,
> The mosses, waters, slaps, and styles,
> That lie between us and our hame — — —
>
> (5–9)

This in turn is put in focus by the opening *descriptio* of the town on market day. It is central to Burns's intention that we should move almost imperceptibly from the plain to the grotesquely heroic, both of which are present in the opening paragraph, one in the lowness of the diction, the other in the epic method of the style.

Much more might be added in illustration of the thesis. *Tam o' Shanter* follows the precepts of the best theorists in having a moral which, like that of *The Rape of the Lock*, is expressed with a certain ambiguity. The Muse is referred to. Epic figures of speech are to be found; for instance, apostrophe:—

> Inspiring bold *John Barleycorn*!
> What dangers thou canst make us scorn!
> Wi' tippeny, we fear nae evil;
> Wi' usquabae, we'll face the devil!
>
> (105–108)

(The echo here of Psalm 23[19] is grotesquely appropriate to Tam's situation.) Simile is common, and of particular interest are the two occasions on which bees are mentioned – once during the inn scene, and once at the beginning of the pursuit. The ultimate source of both figures is Book IV of the *Georgics*, the book which Virgil devoted to the care of bees, and which for the seventeenth and eighteenth centuries was the supreme achievement of the mock-heroic:—

> *Hi motus animorum atque haec certamina tanta*
> *Pulveris exigui iactu compressa quiescent*[20]
>
> (86–87)

Each of these points might be treated at length, but for the present it is sufficient that two facts have been established; the complexities of *Tam o' Shanter* within the classical traditions of the European Enlightenment, and the novelty of the treatment given by Burns, as Scots peasant and man of letters, to the tradition as it already existed. It is insufficient to discuss *Tam o' Shanter* from a purely Scottish point of view, as insufficient as to discuss it as a European or English phenomenon.

So far the second might seem the greater danger; the analysis almost presupposes a Burns who, although he happened to write in Scots, was essentially a European poet of the eighteenth century. For this too, I believe, a good partial case might be made, particularly if the critic restricted his attention to the Kilmarnock volume which appeared in 1786, a volume in which satire, as discussed above, is the characteristic kind; epistle, elegy and epigram the characteristic forms. Burns's ambition to write a Scottish *Georgics* fits this scheme, and is in some limited measure satisfied by that often underestimated poem, *The Vision*.[21]

Although it is earlier than the letter to Mrs Dunlop already quoted, Burns's praise of Ayrshire comes very close to the praise of Italy in *Georgics* II:—

> Here, rivers in the sea were lost;
> There, mountains to the skies were tost:
> Here, tumbling billows mark'd the coast,
>   With surging foam;
> There, distant shone, *Art's* lofty boast,
>   The lordly dome.
>
> Here, Doon pour'd down his far-fetch'd floods;
> There, well-fed Irwine stately thuds:
> Auld, hermit Aire staw thro' his woods,
>   On to the shore;
> And many a lesser torrent scuds,
>   With seeming roar.
>
> Low, in a sandy valley spread,
> An ancient Borough rear'd her head;
> Still, as in *Scottish Story* read,
>   She boasts a *Race*,
> To ev'ry nobler virtue bred,
>   And polish'd grace.
>
>   (72–90)

With this, and much of the remainder of the poem, compare the famous:—

> *Adde tot egregias urbes operumque laborem,*
> *tot congesta manu praeruptis oppida saxis*
> *fluminaque antiquos subterlabentia muros.*
> *an mare quod supra memorem, quodque adluit infra?*
> *anne lacus tantos? te, Lari maxime, teque*
> *fluctibus et fremitu adsurgens Benace marino?*
> *an memorem portus Lucrinoque addita claustra*
> *atque indignatum magnis stridoribus aequor,*
> *Iulia qua ponto longe sonat unda refuso*
> *Tyrrhenusque fretis inmittitur aestus Avernis?*
> *haec eadem argenti rivos aerisque metalla*
> *ostendit venis atque auro plurima fluxit.*
>
> *haec genus acre virum, Marsos, pubemque Sabellam*
> *adsuetumque malo Ligurem Volscosque verutos*
> *extulit, haec Decios Marios magnosque Camillos,*
> *Scipiadas duros bello et te, maxime Caesar,*
> *qui nunc extremis Asiae iam victor in oris*
> *imbellem avertis Romanis arcibus Indum.*
>
> *Salve, magna parens frugum, Saturnia tellus,*
> *magna virum: tibi res antiquae laudis et artis*
> *ingredior sanctos ausus recludere fontes,*
> *Ascraeumque cano Romana per oppida carmen*
> (Georgics ii, 155–176)[22]

In *Tam o' Shanter*, however, if classicism were all the truth, the relation between the honest and the heroic Tam would be straightforward – the honest genuine and the heroic an illusion, exploded by the proximity of the honest. The effect in fact is different, largely as a result of the presence of one character whose function, so far as I am aware, has not often been discussed – Tam's wife, Kate. She appears in the first paragraph as an unnamed archetype, brooding like a storm outside the inn. Her advice and her prophecy occupy the whole of the third paragraph. Mainly it is concerned with drink and male friendship – the miller and the smith to whom in the main narrative corresponds the figure of Souter Johnny. But her last outburst is significant – Tam has drunk with women cronies as well as men, and on a Sunday too:—

> at the L – d's house, even on Sunday,
> Thou drank wi' Kirkton Jean till Monday
> (27–28)

(Compare in the main narrative, the relation of Tam with the landlord's wife:—

> The landlady and *Tam* grew gracious,
> Wi' favours, secret, sweet, and precious.
>
> (47–48))

The combination of drink, women and Sabbath-breaking leads to Kate's prophecy (again a mock-heroic feature) which is so relevant to the remainder of the poem:—

> She prophesied that late or soon,
> Thou would be found deep drown'd in Doon;
> Or catch'd wi' warlocks in the mirk,
> By *Alloway*'s auld haunted kirk
>
> (29–32)

In epic fashion, the prophecy is partly true, partly false. Tam is neither drowned nor catched, and it is not primarily male warlocks who try to catch him; it is witches – women. Satan and women (other women, that is) are particularly associated in Kate's mind, and the imagery of the poem.

"Honest" Tam is in fact a hen-pecked husband who, most of the time, submits meekly to his wife's homilies. This, it is implied, is a consequence of his honesty, which at home entails a loss both of virility and vitality. Both return at the inn; they are partly quenched by the storm, but at Kirk Alloway, to the music of Satan, both return in full strength.

Nannie, the young witch so strikingly developed from the anonymous figure of the prose narrative, is the centre of Tam's heroic vision, in her pathos, emphasized by Professor Daiches[23], as well as in her strength and sensual provocativeness. She is Kate's opposite:—

> Her cutty sark, o' Paisley harn,
> That while a lassie she had worn,
> In longitude tho' sorely scanty,
> It was her best, and she was vauntie. –
> Ah! little kend thy reverend grannie,
> That sark she coft for her wee Nannie,
> Wi' twa pund Scots, ('twas a' her riches),
> Wad ever grac'd a dance of witches!
> But here my Muse her wing maun cour;
> Sic flights are far beyond her pow'r –

> To sing how Nannie lap and flang,
> (A souple jade she was, and strang);
> And how *Tam* stood, like ane bewitch'd,
> And thought his very een enrich'd.
>
> (171–184)

At the same time, Tam remains in the storm, outside the revelry, and when he attempts to intervene, he ceases to be a hero:—

> Till first ae caper, syne anither,
> *Tam* tint his reason a' thegither,
> And roars out, 'Weel done, Cutty-sark!'
> And in an instant all was dark.
>
> (187–190)

Tam's flight towards the river is a rejection of the potentially heroic in favour of honesty, and there is a more or less conscious symbolism in the final loss of Maggie's tale. Tam has escaped, but he has finally lost the virility which he almost recovered at the Kirk: the poem ends with a castration symbol.

When the genuine heroic, as opposed to the false glory of the inn, momentarily enters the poem, it is at the expense of the honest ideal. Equally it is as much opposed to the conventionally heroic as was Tam's original honesty. The heroic is also the Satanic, which rejects all conventions of respectably burgess society. A prose approximation to these ideas is to be found in the letter (No. 114[24]) which Burns wrote from Mauchline to William Nicol, the Edinburgh schoolmaster, on 18th June, 1787. Burns had just returned from Edinburgh by way of the Borders:—

"I never, my friend, thought Mankind very capable of anything generous; but the stateliness of the Patricians in Edin^r, and the servility of my plebeian brethren, who perhaps formerly eyed me askance, since I returned home, have nearly put me out of conceit altogether with my species. – I have bought a pocket Milton, which I carry perpetually about with me, in order to study the sentiments – the dauntless magnanimity; the intrepid unyielding independance; the desperate daring, and noble defiance of hardship, in that great personage, Satan. – 'Tis true, I have just now a little cash; but I am afraid the damn'd star that hitherto has shed its malignant, purpose-blasting rays full in my zenith; that noxious Planet so baneful in its influences to the rhyming tribe, I must dread it is not yet beneath my horizon. – Misfortune [dogs] the path of human life; the poetic mind finds itself miserably deranged in, and unfit for the walks of business; add to all that, thoughtless follies and harebrained whims, like so many Ignes fatui, eternally diverging from the right line of sober discretion, sparkle with step-bewitching blaze in the idly-gazing eyes of the poor heedless Bard, till, pop, 'he falls like Lucifer, never to hope again.' – God grant this may be an unreal picture with respect to me!"

From the final clauses, it is clear that Burns associated both the stateliness of the Patricians and the servility of the Plebs with the walks of business – of commercial life, that is to say – and that both were opposed to the Miltonic Satan, who was identified with "the poor heedless Bard". The opposition is at least partially recurrent. Compare, in *The Vision*:—

> All in this mottie, misty clime,
> I backward mus'd on wasted time,
> How I had spent my *youthfu' prime*,
>   An' done nae-thing,
> But stringing blethers up in rhyme
>   For fools to sing.
>
> Had I to guid advice but harket,
> I might, by this, hae led a market,
> Or strutted in a Bank and clarket
>   My *Cash-Account*;
> While here, half-mad, half-fed, half-sarket,
>   Is a' th'amount.
>
> I started, mutt'ring blockhead! coof!
> And heav'd on high my wauket loof,
> To swear by a' yon starry roof,
>   Or some rash aith,
> That I, henceforth, would be *rhyme-proof*
>   Till my last breath –
>
>   (19–35)

The oath is prevented by the Muse of Ayrshire, Coila, a heraldic figure who possesses several features in common with Nannie in *Tam o' Shanter*, and indeed, granted some essential and obvious differences, with Burns as he represents himself in the letter to Nicol:—

> When click! the *string* the *snick* did draw;
> And jee! the door gaed to the wa';
> And by my ingle-lowe I saw,
>   Now bleezan bright,

A tight, outlandish *Hizzie*, braw,
    Come full in sight — — —

A 'hare-brain'd, sentimental trace'
Was strongly marked in her face;
A wildly-witty, rustic grace
    Shone full upon her
Her *eye*, ev'n turn'd on empty space,
    Beam'd keen with *Honor*.

Down flow'd her robe, a *tartan* sheen,
Till half a leg was scrimply seen;
And such a *leg*! my bonie Jean
    Could only peer it;
Sae straught, sae taper, tight and clean,
    Nane else came near it.
             (37–42: 55–66)

Coila however still represents society, albeit a society more heroic, more primitive and natural, and so more akin to poetry than that in which Burns found himself. The figures commemorated on her mantle belong to the ancient families of Ayrshire, especially the Wallaces and the Montgomeries, and correspond to Virgil's *Decios, Marios, magnosque Camillos/Scipiadas duros bello*. When the perspective extends beyond "this mottie, misty clime", the style preserves decorum by modulating to high-middle and high from the low-middle to low of the subdued opening. The epic sweep which Burns was attempting is also indicated by the heroic Ossianic word "Duan" which he applied to his cantos. In a selfishly commercial society, the poet is necessarily oppressed, but his real kinship is with the natural, the noble and the heroic, which provide his comfort.

In Coila, however, there is no overt trace of the Satanic. And indeed it is not for anything normally understood as Satanic that Burns in many of his poems rejected society, except in so far as the Satanic for him had come to represent the free and the passionate, Satanic only to the extent that it is opposed to the capitalism and Calvinism of the Auld Lichts and their brethren. Elsewhere he gives it the name of Liberty. To this extent, too, Nannie, the witches and Satan himself are partially inadequate symbols — a fact which Carlyle recognized but over-emphasized in his early review of Lockhart's *The Life of Robert Burns*. Burns, he says[25], in *Tam o' Shanter*, "has not gone back, much less carried us back, into that dark, earnest, wondering age, when the tradition was believed, and when it took its rise; he does not attempt, by any new-modelling of his supernatural ware, to strike anew that deep mysterious chord of human nature, which once responded to such things; and which lives in us too, and will forever live, though silent now, or vibrating with far other notes, and to far different issues." It was no part of Burns's intention, of course, to attempt any such thing; the poem is mock-heroic and a product of the Enlightenment, with as one of its side products a demonstration of one method by which apparently supernatural phenomena might be explained away. Burns adopts the same posture in "Address to the Deil":—

> When twilight did my *Graunie* summon,
> To say her pray'rs, douse, honest woman,
> Aft 'yont the dyke she's heard you bumman,
>   Wi' eerie drone;
> Or, rustling, thro' the boortries coman,
>   Wi' heavy groan.
>
> Ae dreary, windy, winter night,
> The stars shot down wi' sklentan light,
> Wi' you, *mysel*, I gat a fright
>   Ayont the lough;
> Ye, like a rash-buss, stood in sight
>   Wi' waving sugh:
>
> The cudgel in my nieve did shake,
> Each bristl'd hair stood like a stake,
> When wi' an eldritch, stoor *quaick, quaick*,
>   Amang the springs,
> Awa ye squatter'd like a *drake*,
>   On whistling wings.
>
>   (31–48)

This in turn may be related to the autobiographical letter (No. 125[26]) which Burns wrote to Dr John Moore on 2nd August, 1787:—

"In my infant and boyish days too, I owed much to an old Maid of my Mother's, remarkable for her ignorance, credulity and superstition. – She had, I suppose, the largest collection in the county of tales and songs concerning devils, ghosts, fairies, brownies, witches, warlocks, spunkies, kelpies, elf-candles, deadlights, wraiths, apparitions, cantraips, giants, inchanted towers, dragons and other trumpery. – This cultivated the latent seeds of Poesy; but had so strong an effect on my imagination, that to this hour, in my nocturnal rambles, I

sometimes keep a sharp look-out in suspicious places; and
though nobody can be more sceptical in these matters than I, yet
it often takes an effort of Philosophy to shake off these idle
terrors."

Notable here is the connection of superstition and credulity with "the
latent seeds of Poesy". Burns is saying, not that poetry is identical with
these, but rather that the imaginative freedom and range, the suspension
of disbelief and imaginative juxtaposition of opposites characteristic of
poetry, has something in common with, and may find material in, scientifically and philosophically invalid survivals; that a background of
superstitious belief can offer a mind eventually powerful enough to see
through absurdity, the best preparation for ultimate poetic success. Some
undesirable side-effects remain, but in later life poetry and philosophy
can exist harmoniously together. *Address to the Deil* and *Tam o' Shanter*, in
different ways, are examples. In the first, the poetry derives, not from the
implied scepticism, nor from the underlying superstition but from the
fusion of three elements, seen in relation to the idea of Satan: the external
natural landscape, the romantic shudder and the scientific comment of
the poet. *Tam o' Shanter* is more elaborate, but not basically different,
especially when one considers the number of ways in which it is possible
for a mare to lose her tail. *Tam o' Shanter* nevertheless is not so much a
rationalistic poem as "Address to the Deil"; the difference of effect, as I
have suggested, is probably to be found in the vigour and sexual
challenge of Nannie to which in the other poem there is no equivalent.

It is by way of Nannie and the witches that *Tam o' Shanter* is linked to
the poem which Carlyle was the first to regard as Burns's greatest
achievement[27], *Love and Liberty*, better known still as *The Jolly Beggars*[28].
Like the witches, the beggars have rejected society. Burns however
could believe in beggary with an intensity which was impossible for him
when he wrote on the supernatural; it was a daily fact of agricultural life
in the eighteenth century, and on occasions he was himself close to
beggary. Out of context, the concluding chorus of *Love and Liberty* may
seem swaggering and false:—

> A fig for those by Law protected,
> Liberty's a glorious feast!
> Courts for Cowards were erected,
> Churches built to please the Priest
> (277–281)

In context the effect is very different. The beggar has become the type of
the natural man, "the thing itself", transcending even the dance of the

witches in the storm in *Tam o' Shanter*. The intensity is heightened by the elaborate and courtly stanza form adopted with complete mastery for the *recitativo*:—

> When lyart leaves bestrow the yird,
> Or wavering like the Bauckie-bird,
>   Bedim cauld Boreas' blast;
> When hailstanes drive wi' bitter skyte,
> And infant Frosts begin to bite,
>   In hoary cranreuch drest;
> Ae night at e'en a merry core
>   O' randie, gangrel bodies,
> In Poose-Nansie's held the splore,
>   To drink their orra dudies:
>   Wi' quaffing, and laughing
>   They ranted an' they sang;
>   Wi' jumping, an' thumping,
>   The vera girdle rang.
>
> First, niest the fire, in auld, red rags,
> Ane sat; weel brac'd wi' mealy bags,
>   And knapsack a' in order;
> His doxy lay within his arm;
> Wi' Usquebae an' blankets warm,
>   She blinket on her Sodger:
> An' ay he gies the tozie drab
>   The tither skelpan kiss,
> While she held up her greedy gab,
>   Just like an aumous dish:
> Ilk smack still, did crack still,
>   Just like a cadger's whip,
> Then staggering, an' swaggering,
>   He roar'd this ditty up.
>
> (1–28)

In Chapter III of Part I of *Gulliver's Travels*[29], Swift describes one of the amusements of the Court of Lilliput:—

> "The Emperor had a mind one Day to entertain me with several of the Country Shows: wherein they exceed all Nations I have known, both for Dexterity and Magnificence. I was diverted with none so much as that of the Rope-Dancers, performed upon a slender white Thread, extended about two Foot, and twelve Inches from the Ground. Upon which, I shall

desire Liberty, with the Reader's Patience, to enlarge a little. This Diversion is only practised by those Persons, who are Candidates for great Employments, and high Favour, at Court. They are trained in this Art from their Youth, and are not always of noble Birth, or of liberal Education. When a great Office is vacant, either by Death or Disgrace (which often happens) five or six of those Candidates petition the Emperor to entertain his Majesty and the Court with a Dance on the Rope; and whoever jumps the highest without falling, succeeds in the Office. Very often the chief Ministers themselves are commanded to shew their skill, and to convince the Emperor that they have not lost their Faculty. Flimnap, The Treasurer, is allowed to cut a Caper on the strait Rope, at least an Inch higher than any other Lord in the whole Empire."

Swift's satire turns on the minute size of the politicians he describes, and on the dangerous pointlessness of the game they attempt. Burns may have remembered this when he wrote the Merry-Andrew scene[30], which probably figured in an early version of *Love and Liberty*:—

> I, ance, was ty'd up like a stirk,
>   For civilly swearing and quaffing;
> I, ance, was abus'd i' the kirk,
>   For towsing a lass i' my daffin.
> Poor Andrew that tumbles for sport,
>   Let nae body name wi' a jeer;
> There's even, I'm tauld, i' the Court
>   A Tumbler ca'd the Premier.
>
> (21–28)

The comparison is significant. Swift left his figures with some rags of dignity – on however diminutive a scale, they are still great Lords performing before an Emperor. Burns's Premier is reduced to the level of an idiot beggar tumbling for the amusement of "randie, gangrel bodies" and their doxies. In the eighteenth century, a literary rejection of the values of society could scarcely go further. Burns here goes beyond the reach of the Enlightenment.

NOTES

1. "Epistle to J. R******"; Kinsley, *Burns*, I.61–62.
2. "To the Same" (i.e. J. Lapraik); Kinsley, *Burns*, I.89–93
3. "To W. S.*****", Kinsley, *Burns*, I.93–98.

4. "The Study of Poetry", *Essays in Criticism. Second Series* (London, 1889), 44.

5. Kinsley, *Burns*, II.557–564.

6. Kinsley, *Burns*, I.145–152.

7. Kinsley, *Burns*, I.168–172.

8. D. F. C. Coldwell (ed.), *Virgil's* Aeneid *Translated into Scottish Verse by Gavin Douglas Bishop of Dunkeld* III (S.T.S., Edinburgh and London, 1959), 1.

9. J. De Lancey Ferguson, *The Letters of Robert Burns* (2 vols., Oxford, 1931), (referred to hereafter as *Letters*), II.22–24.

10. *Letters*, I.221–222.

11. *Letters*, I.106–107.

12. Kinsley, *Burns*, II.762–763.

13. *Augustan Satire: Intention and Idiom in English Poetry 1660–1750*, (Oxford, 1952), 46.

14. *Pope: The Rape of the Lock* (London, 1961), 13.

15. *Robert Burns* (London, 1952), 280–292.

16. *Burns: A Study of the Poems and Songs* (Edinburgh and London, 1960).

17. G. Tillotson, *On the Poetry of Pope* (2nd edit., Oxford, 1950), 49–51.

18. Sargeaunt, *op. cit.*, 90.

19. "Yea, though I walk through the valley of the shadow of death, I will fear no evil" (verse 4).

20. "By scattering a pinch of dust, these passions of the heart and these mighty conflicts will be quelled and grow still."

21. Kinsley, *Burns*, I.103–113.

22. "In addition, there are so many noble cities and public works brought to completion, so many towns hand-raised on steep crags, and rivers gliding beneath ancient walls. Need I mention the seas which wash her coasts above and below, or her mighty lakes – you, giant Como, and you, Garda, surging with a roar like the sea? Need I mention her harbours, and the mole added to the Lucrine lake, and the ocean complaining with huge clamour where the Julian wave resounds far and wide as the waters pour through and the Tyrrhenian tide is channeled into Lake Avernus? This same land has revealed streams of silver and mines of bronze in veins, and has flowed mightily with gold. This land has reared a valiant race of men, the Marsi and the Sabellian youth, the Ligurian trained to hardship and the Volscian spearmen. This land bore the Decii, the Marii, and the great Camilli, the Scipios, men of iron in war, and you, greatest Caesar, who now, already victorious in the farthest parts of Asia, turn away the unwarlike Indian from the citadels of Rome. Hail, great parent of crops and men, Saturnian land! For you I begin themes of ancient praise and art, daring to open the sacred springs of the Muses as I sing the song of Ascra through the towns of the Romans."

23. *Robert Burns*, 290.

24. *Letters*, I.96–97.

25. *Critical and Miscellaneous Essays Collected and Republished* (7 vols., London, 1872), II.23.

26. *Letters*, I.104–116.

27. *Op. cit.*, 23–24.

28. Kinsley, *Burns*, I.195–209.

29. World's Classics edit., 29–30.

30. Kinsley, *Burns*, I.199.

INDEX